Once a Pilgrim
Always a Coach

Praise for *Once a Pilgrim—Always a Coach*

Lynne Burney is a legend in the coaching world. She was one of the first to pursue this profession in France. Her many contributions to the field are wide ranging: from NLP to Clean Coaching techniques which she pioneered in our country. Situated halfway between a travelogue and professional introspection, this book, that has been long awaited will, in all likelihood, rapidly become a classic.

PIERRE BLANC-SAHNOUN, founder of La Fabrique Narrative (Narrative Therapy) and author of *L'art de coacher—Interéditions* (*The Art of Coaching*)

____

If you deal with your reactions to your life events and journeyings as Lynne did, it could change your view of the world and that of yourself.

MAURICE BRASHER, author, translator and Process Work figurehead in France

____

Lynne's marvelous first book will lead you into her life story in authentic ways that will inform and amuse you. Lynne offers you a nuanced analysis of human nature with a sense of humor, understated self-mockery, and coaching insights. I delved into this book with great delight.

BÉNÉDICTE MERCIER, co-president of SODEBO

Lynne floored me with one of her unexpected questions at the end of our first meeting—So what's the added value in continuing to feel guilty?

This question, along with the many more you will find in Lynne's book, will stimulate you into thinking more deeply about your life experience. They may, as they did with me, invite you to pull together the forgotten parts of yourself so that you, like me, will feel more whole and vital.

THOMAS COVILLE, sailor-navigator, holder of the world record round-the-world solo trimaran, Christmas Day 2016

ONCE A PILGRIM ALWAYS A COACH

A journey to the tomb of Saint James

LYNNE BURNEY

LKB PUBLISHING
PARIS, FRANCE

LKB Publishing

Paris, France

Copyright © 2022 by Lynne Burney. All rights reserved.

Cataloging-in-Publication Data is on file with the Library of Congress

Paperback ISBN: 978-2-9584245-0-3

eBook ISBN: 978-2-9584245-1-0

Book design by Christina Thiele

Editorial production by kn literary

www.lkb-coaching.com

Printed in the United States of America

For Richard
much loved fellow traveler
life companion
husband
valuable critic
YBD

Contents

Foreword

What a delight to meet a professional woman who writes a pilgrim's story about her own subjective experience and not another treatise telling us all how to do things better!

Lynne Burney chooses to explore that mysterious inner life we all have but rarely relish and follow as intimately as she does in this journey to the feet of Saint James in Santiago. A journey of four years and three seasons with her life partner, Richard.

There is a subtle invitation here, as she gently stimulates us through simple questions, asking that we participate in this journey with her! And what an invitation, on so many levels. Lynne discovers that her relationship with her partner will change, and that her relationship with her body, especially her feet and legs, will change. We join her as she experiences the varying welcomes of hosts on the path and as she recalls her past: as a child in New Zealand and as a young explorer of new life in Asia, the Middle East, and Europe.

Each memory is a sudden flash of light onto the paradox of life: in one cameo, Lynne describes herself as "enthusiastic, positive, energetic and well dressed"; in another, arriving at her night's lodgings, she "crawled up the four flights of stairs. . . . Once inside the room, I closed the door and declared it my mausoleum."

She remembers sexual harassment in Jerusalem on the most sacred day and in the most sacred place in Christendom. And the strange effect of a French priest whose voice vibrates her into bliss. Life is indeed full of these strange experiences, and Lynne gives us the taste of them without judgment; they are part of her story, but they do not detract from her central theme.

That theme is indeed the effect of the Pilgrim's Way. Following the Way honestly, Lynne also takes us into those moments when the ordinary becomes extraordinary; when multicolored butterflies awaken her to life itself. Or, as she puts it, when "the self that fragments over the course of an ordinary day slides graciously back into the wholeness. A sense of completeness permeates the entire system, where all is included, whence all life flows."

So to you, the reader, I hope that your journey with Lynne through so many landscapes and on so many levels will fill you with awe and delight at this amazing pilgrimage that we are all on, with its heights and its depths, its fears and its sacredness. May you find your way on your own unique journey, inspired by Lynne's—

one that took her from a desire to do something new and exciting, to finding why pilgrims have traveled paths to visit sacred places for countless centuries.

Enjoy the journey!

Jennifer de Gandt
Coaching elder and therapist
NLP & Clean Language Pioneer in France

Introduction

The story begins just before Easter in the year 2000.

In February, my life partner, Richard, suggested that we walk the Way of Saint James. I said yes instantly, without forethought: no hesitation. It sounded thoughtless even to me, but it was a yes that came from deep within. The kind of yes that promised no regret. I would have been incapable of explaining the whys and wherefores of my answer then. It would take over 1,800 kilometers of walking for me to recognize where my yes came from, and that it would be a life changer.

When Richard popped the question, I was unaware of why people went on pilgrimages. I would discover that some walked to seek redemption, or to find companionship or sex or adventure or all three; that others sought an antidote to the emptiness of city life or wished to take on a challenge; and that still others followed the Way because they needed a holiday or needed to belong or needed to love.

PART 1 FRANCE
Sur les Pas de St Jacques
CONQUES
2000 SPRING

Setting Out

On April 14, a week before Easter, we touched down at Rodez airport in central southern France. Our attire may have raised the odd eyebrow given that we were on the early morning business flight out of Orly, but otherwise we were just another middle-aged couple flying in from the capital, ostensibly to begin a walking tour. I had had a few coaching clients the day before we left, and Richard, a journalist, had completed an article he had been writing for *L'Express*. It was pretty much business as usual, just another event in a busy calendar year. It was good to take time off, do something different, get a bit of excitement in the form of the unknown: an adventure—no apparent connection to the startling yes of February.

I was well dressed for the occasion: elegant light gray walking trousers that unzipped down to shorts, quick-dry, color-coordinated shirt, dark brown leather sun hat that would work in the Australian outback or on a Paris boulevard, and a compact new backpack I had bought based on advice offered in the latest guidebooks. No one would have been aware of how carefully Richard had packed and repacked his backpack; nor would anyone have immediately noticed the little extras I had added to mine: the just-in-case essentials like body cream, perfume, and something nice to put on in the evening. Tea didn't count as an extra.

My boots were not new. I had worn them on many hikes over the past twenty years. They were made of soft brown leather, reinforced at the ankles, and they were definitely ready to go.

So we were standing in a nearly empty airport in Rodez ready to begin the adventure when I remembered we needed water. Luckily, bottled spring water was available over the counter, so there was no immediate challenge to my role as "medieval pilgrim on the road to Santiago"—what a pilgrim in the twenty-first century was like had no shape or size in my mind as I set out from the airport. I had this vague feeling that a genuine pilgrim would have thought of water as the most essential part of her equipment, but then I also thought she probably would not have taken a plane to Rodez, either. In reality I didn't give any of this much thought. I was at the beginning of something: enthusiastic, positive, energetic, and well dressed.

We set out at a good stride. Richard walked ahead. We later invested in a pedometer so we could keep track of the distances we were covering, but on that first day, over country tracks and trails, I had no idea how far we had gone until I realized I was having difficulty keeping up with Richard. That was already a new experience.

I was a businesswoman well familiar with the demands of running a small operation and maintaining a large network, but my state of mind at the beginning of this pilgrimage resembled that of a young child expecting to be shown the delights of the French countryside. It peeved me to have to get on with the walking and manage it on my own. I tried to keep myself amused, and interested in the unchanging landscape, but, like a child, I felt I wanted some entertainment at some point.

I did maintain a good rhythm that first morning. The sun shone—an unimpeded blue in a noonday sky. The breeze was fresh, and signs of spring peeped above the earth in pert yellows and shy reds.

About lunchtime it was clear to me that I had no idea where I was going. Lack of investment in the planning phase was the obvious explanation. It wouldn't have mattered had I not started to feel weary and disgruntled. I was in love with the romance of following a medieval trail to the tomb of Saint James in Spain, as so many well-meaning feet had done since the Middle Ages. But now that my muscles and bones were actually engaged in the project, the fifty-year-old wanted times, distances, and an ETA. The adult realized that she needed to measure her effort. She absolutely needed to know where she was going to spend that first night. Santiago was one thing, and that was likely years ahead; the first night was another.

Despite my resounding initial yes, I had entrusted all the logistics to Richard. I had slipped easily and willingly into "little girl" happy to follow "Dad" on an adventure. Richard fell just as easily into his preferred roles of dad and planner. All was well until it wasn't and I wanted answers to a few practical questions. Had I not abdicated all responsibility for the planning of this first stage of the pilgrimage, I would have known that we were going to Marcillac, and that it was a twenty-six-kilometer walk from the Rodez airport. I may even have been able to pace myself over that first day on the road. But I knew nothing and had done nothing to change that.

It wasn't the first time in my life an abdication of responsibility had gotten me into trouble. The headmistress of Christchurch Girls' High had once devoted an entire morning's assembly of over five hundred students to the subject of "responsibility" and had ended with a request for Lynne Burney to report to her office immediately. I was severely reprimanded in the privacy of her office about my responsibility, as a team captain, to forgo pleasures like playing basketball with friends and instead attend training sessions. The coach, I was told, had been most unhappy. I left the headmistress's office riddled with guilt and full of promises to mend my ways. I never dared say that I thought the coach was a dolt and I didn't like her training techniques. She must have known, and this was her revenge!

My lack of dedication to logistics, and the ease with which I was willing to trust that all would be well despite scanty planning, manifested itself early in my relationship with Richard, and in my career. Once, I took a suburban train to get to Caen, in the north of France. I had a professional engagement and was focused on the work ahead, not on how to get there. It was winter. It was dark. I was on my own. I had three heavy bags. I knew I had to change trains somewhere after leaving the main station in Paris. I had not written down the name of the village where I was to transfer to Caen. I spoke French quite well, but I wasn't certain I had heard well when the name of the station where I thought I had to change was announced. I was close to panic as the doors of the carriage started to close. I made a snap decision, tossed the bags onto the platform, threw myself between the sliding doors, and landed on a cold concrete slab. I watched the train pull away slowly, and then the night swallowed me up. It was freezing. The wind increased the chill factor by several degrees. I was afraid and furious at the same time. My supreme Kiwi confidence in myself was shaken to its roots by a French reality.

I located a telephone box despite the blackness of the night, found some coins in my purse, called Richard, burst into tears, tried to pronounce the name of the station written on a signpost at the end of the platform and between sobs, told him I was utterly lost and hadn't a clue what to do. He drove through the night to find me, picked me up, and drove me a further two hours to my destination. I felt foolish and guilty and thankful. I did a great job professionally the following day, but I swore I would get someone else to organize travel the next time.

So in many ways not knowing or remembering where we were staying that first night of our journey to Santiago was par for the course. I liked being able to rely on Richard to determine each day's destination. There was no doubt something deeply satisfying in feeling taken care of—of not being the eldest. My child played to his father. This game would not be without consequences.

"We are going to Marcillac," Richard said when I finally asked him. He could have said "Timbuktu" and I would have been just as wise! The afternoon wore on. My feet hurt. My backpack was too heavy. My keen beginning was now just a hard slog. I needed to know in very precise terms how much farther we had to go. Without the numbers, I had no language to sweet-talk my body with—at least until Marcillac. The pain in my middle-aged body shook me again and again back into my adult self. I was no child out for a trot in the park. The adventure would not be just a fun outing. I could not leave everything to Richard if I wanted this to be something we shared. He loved to plan, and I loved to do. We would need to find ways of respecting each other's preferred way of functioning while sharing tasks as two consenting adults.

When you set out on a journey, what is most important to you?

Does anything change if the journey is a shared one?

Marcillac

We arrived at our first night's lodgings to a scowling innkeeper with a bulbous nose. Richard had booked in advance, and it was too late in the day to change accommodations in such a small town. I had been imagining a beaming publican ready to offer succor to the weary traveler along the road to Saint James. I wasn't expecting him to wash my feet, but I thought that he might have something in the fridge, and that the television would work. He muttered a few unpleasantries, pushed our room key across a sticky bar top, and growled, "Pas de television dans les chambres"—no TV in the rooms!

When did an expectation you had bump into reality?

What happened next?

Suddenly, the whole idea of Santiago seemed foolish in the extreme: walking hundreds of miles in every kind of weather to visit a big cathedral in a foreign town where thousands would be gathering to see a statue of one of the apostles, James, bearing a scallop shell. And this is what I would spend weeks of my holiday time doing. *WHAT?*

The bad-tempered innkeeper was a harbinger of the many assumptions that would be challenged on multiple occasions on the way to Santiago. Time and time again, what I had *imagined* bore no resemblance to what *was*. I would have the choice of holding on to my preferred version of reality or accepting a different version. The less fraught version of innkeeper reality was that some were grumpy and some were not.

We left ours behind in his state of grumpiness and walked out into the cool Marcillac evening to find a place to eat, looking through windows and reading outdoor menu boards. The restaurant we chose felt warm and friendly. There were quite a few tables already occupied, but we were shown to a cozy corner. The fare was simple—mostly local produce offered up in traditional recipes: farmhouse chicken with stewed tomatoes, local sausage with mashed potatoes, salads with homemade vinaigrette. The owner's open, smiling face contrasted dramatically with our innkeeper's snarling features and made us feel especially welcome. He warmed to us on hearing that we were walking the Way of Saint James, as he had done himself. It was he who taught us the two questions that would be our companions for the rest of the journey. Where have you come from today? and Where are you going tomorrow?

No one would ever ask what I did for a living. People might talk about their hopes and dreams or about their dysfunctional families, but never about their social status. These were two questions that stripped life down to its bare bones, that stated without saying that all were equal in their aspiration to walk the Way. They assumed that all people had a past and all had a future, and that they were alive in that moment to answer. They were questions without rank or conflict embedded in them. In short, they were safe questions for any stranger along a lonely road.

> **Where have you come from today?**
>
> **Where are you going tomorrow?**
>
> **How do these two questions resonate with you?**

The restaurateur's smile and questions welcomed us into the bearers-of-scallop-shell-and-Credencial-del-Peregrino club. The credencial, which bears the mark of the scallop shell, symbol of Saint James, is a pilgrim's passport that gets stamped at each evening's resting place. On arrival at the Pilgrim's Reception Office in Santiago, it is presented as proof of pilgrimage. Once approved by this official body, the pilgrim is given a certificate ("Compostela") acknowledging that he has walked a minimum of a hundred kilometers to complete the pilgrimage. The credencial must be placed in your hands by a recognized organization before you set out. You do not have to be a Christian to receive it, but it comes into your hands as a recommendation to future hosts that you are a bona fide seeker of the divine. It is not a rite of passage but rather a statement of good intention.

On this first night in Marcillac, it was a meaningless and unstamped document folded concertina-style inside my over-the-shoulder wallet holder. I would learn to eat and sleep with it over the next four years of intermittent wandering.

Conques

The following morning, we set off for Conques. I had no idea where Conques was situated on the map of France, but at least, on the dawn of that second day of the journey, I knew where we were headed. The novelty of the adventure had worn off. Neither my body nor my mind was as fresh as it had been only twenty-four hours previously. I was alone again with my thoughts, moving at four kilometers an hour in one direction with a mind moving at breakneck speed in all directions. There was nothing to interfere with the tedium of cows in fields, chewing grass. I tried singing out loud but rapidly exhausted my repertoire, so I repeated the songs in different modes. I did nursery rhyme, opera, rock, gospel, and country versions of old Beatles numbers. "Hey Jude" revealed hidden dimensions under my doctoring.

I remembered the family get-togethers in my grand-mother's day when everyone clustered around the piano for a good ol' singalong.

Time passed.

Slowly.

Around lunchtime we were up on a plateau. We had had to clamber up a hillside, through scrubby woodland alongside a trickle of water, to reach this flat expanse of land with a village on the top. When you are on foot, flat is always quite an attractive proposition. And it was now, even if the village itself was not a particularly memorable event.

Small two-story houses lined both sides of the main road. The pungent aroma of espresso and French cigarettes wafting out a front door made the only café in town easy to find. We were glad to stop there out of the wind and to order two baguettes with ham and cheese. Chewing was tedious but less so than watching cows do it. I was at least getting nourishment—walking fuel. Replenishment. Bovines chewing all day were boring beasts. But that had been all that was available to take my mind off the endless repetition of putting one foot in front of the other. The café was a welcome change of scenery.

An idea, born of fatigue, boredom, and a growing desire to be there rather than spend time getting there, started to take shape in my mind. *Let's hitch a ride,* I thought.

Years later, when, through a lot of meditation practice, I had become more skilled at watching the way my mind operates, I could catch an idea before it wedded itself to me. I could save myself some of the pain of a divorce. But at that instant in time, I was, for whatever reason, hitched to my idea.

Have you ever watched the way thoughts arise in your mind?

What do you notice first?

What happens when you begin to notice?

And then what happens?

Thought became deed, and we stood at the roadside for a good forty minutes. Not a single car or truck went by. We never even had a chance to put our thumbs out. It was as if the universe had ordered a moratorium on all motorized vehicles. The spring sun was still weak, and there was a coolish breeze that promised to chill us as we stood there waiting on the car-free road, which sliced through the village center. Even though it had been my idea to hitchhike, I was beginning to have second thoughts. I swung my head from side to side, willing a vehicle to appear, but no amount of peering down the road either way produced any sign of transport. I adjusted my backpack, glanced down at my soft brown walking boots, and thought, *Hitching's a no-go. Have feet, must walk. It's the deal.* I looked at Richard. He looked at me.

I said, "Pilgrims walk, right?"

He said, "That's right."

"So are we pilgrims on the Way to Saint James?

"We are."

"Not just a couple of old hippies on a hitchhiking holiday in France?"

"Nope."

And it was at that precise moment, on that second day of the pilgrimage, that we agreed to the first of our only two ground rules: we would walk the Way until our feet could walk no farther, and there we would stop, regardless of the target we had set ourselves; and then we would go home, and carry on from the same spot the following year.

Later, when we realized that carrier firms were

available to transport backpacks from one lodging to the next, we set our second ground rule: we would carry our own backpacks, and if either one of our backs could no longer support the weight, we would stop and return home, then continue from where we'd left off on renewed feet and with stronger backs the following year.

This simple but rigorous framework gave me not only a firm resolve to go the distance but also a way to show gentle respect toward what I was asking of my body. Much later, this self-imposed rule would be seriously challenged, and my personal determination would exclude all form of gentleness toward anyone else.

When you set out on a journey, what do you want, need, or expect from others?

What makes the journey difficult for you? Easy for you?

After we had given up on the idea of hitchhiking, I slipped into a dreary trudge along a never-ending trail that wound continually upward. Dust covered my boots. My calf muscles screamed. I rounded one bend after another. Richard was nowhere in sight. My mind was locked into an exhausting game: hope, just before rounding a bend; then despair on actually rounding it to find yet another bend in front of me.

On and on.

Endless.

When I was eight years old, I contracted rheumatic fever. Before anyone knew what was wrong with me, the joints in my legs had swollen, making walking difficult for me. I was hobbling through town with my mother, her aunt, and her mother—my Nana. We were on holiday in Dunedin, in the South Island of New Zealand, where my mother's aunt lived. I was feeling very sorry for myself and complained that I could not run and dance like other kids. My mother's much-beloved aunt turned to me and said in a very sharp manner that I should keep my eyes on the stars and never hang my head. The other two women supported her, and I was given to understand that we women did not complain about pain. We women marched with our eyes heavenward.

I never forgot. But I did stay in bed at home for four months, consuming vast quantities of penicillin and iron. The family doctor had not diagnosed a streptococcal infection correctly, so there was a risk of permanent damage to my heart. Heart disease was part of the family heritage on my father's side. I did not complain. I learned to go the distance. The women in my mother's family taught me the art of sticking with it.

I rounded a bend and saw Richard seated at the foot of a giant stone cross, his gaze directed somewhere far in the distance. I felt a burst of boundless joy. I didn't know what he was looking at, but his posture said that we had arrived. No more bends. Respite. A hint of those stars that my mother's aunt was alluding to when she admonished my eight-year-old self for being downcast. Grace to those who walk the Way.

I sat down beside Richard and let my gaze join his. And there it was, Conques, perched on a hillside in all its medieval splendor. With the day's destination in full view, I cared little for the pain in my legs or my back. It mattered even less that we had to descend deep down into the valley and then follow a sinuous overgrown track along the valley floor before making our way up the other side of the mountain to reach the age-old gates to the town. It was hell, but I did not complain.

I don't remember how many stone steps we had to climb from the outer walls of the town to the inner walls and then on to the ancient center of the town, but I do remember groaning ostentatiously when the publican announced cheerfully that our room was on the fourth floor.

"No lift," he added with a grin.

I literally crawled up the four flights of stairs on all fours. Once inside the room, I closed the door and declared it my mausoleum. It was the one final effort of the day that did me in. There was no way I was going to go downstairs in search of food. No way I would make it up the stairs again, even if I managed to get all the way down in the first place. I was utterly wiped out. We women do not complain about the pain.

But we are not daft either.

Sleep first.

Food later.

Palm Sunday

The following day was Palm Sunday. There were services at the abbey of Sainte-Foy. I was not really a tourist, but I wasn't exactly a pilgrim yet, either. I was Christian but not Catholic. I wore boots, not shoes, but my aches felt legitimate enough for me to attend the 11:00 a.m. service with Richard.

We sat halfway down the aisle on the right, in the center of a pew. We hardly stood out among the crowds of locals and passing-through pilgrims. The priest wore a long white robe and, supported by several other similarly clad fellows, called all travelers of the Way forward to receive a piece of bread, a special blessing, and a prayer for divine protection. I didn't dare step forward, and it wasn't the right time to check church law on who could and couldn't receive the bread, the blessing, or both.

There was only one time I dared to do that: I was celebrating an interreligious dialogue weekend at an ashram outside Paris. It was another Sunday morning, and it was the Catholic priest's turn to lead a small mass inside the meditation chapel. The chapel was decorated with portraits of Ramakrishna, Sarada Devi, and Swami Vivekananda. There were flowers in abundance, and most participants were seated, yogi-like, on cushions on the carpeted floor.

When the priest asked, with an enigmatic smile, whether we felt Christ's love for us, I could honestly raise my hand in affirmation. He then called everyone forward to accept Christ's body and blood. I saw everyone else moving forward with the automated ease of people who had grown up in the predominantly Catholic culture of France. I had a moment of panic and called out, "Is it okay for me to accept the bread if I have not been baptized in the Catholic Church?" Time stopped. Smiles froze. Suspended breath can be quite long for a yogi. The priest, caught in the magnanimous nature of the weekend of multireligious dialogue, beamed at me and said, "I'll have to check that one with my archbishop." He beckoned me forward.

But the Palm Sunday service in the abbey of Sainte-Foy just was not the time or the place to have an ecumenical debate. Richard, soon to be a divorcé, was struggling with what was kosher behavior under the circumstances, so I hissed in his ear, "Go get the bread!"

He did, and I know he didn't regret the move.

He was a Catholic baptized into the tradition. I wasn't. While religious ritual fascinated me, I felt free from religious indoctrination and tried to respect other people's practices.

Looking back, I see now that when those rituals are performed with a truly open heart, there is enough room in them to include all traditions, all religions, and all cultures. I like to think the Palm Sunday service in the abbey was one of those rituals.

In a nook inside the church stood a small wooden statue of Saint James with a scallop shell chiseled into the wide brim of his hat. I would return to this spot five years later and be overcome with tears of gratitude, but on that second day, and from inside an aching body, I was simply looking out. Curious. Waiting. Watching.

Does the word "pilgrim" have any meaning in your life today?

Fueled by the picturesque beauty of medieval Conques, the service, and the throngs of people, our fully rested legs carried us easily over to the other side of the mountain to the industrial wasteland of Decazeville.

Decazeville had thrived during the Industrial Revolution. Coal mines and steel factories had grown up there. But there were no vestiges of an industrial history. And there were no visual signs of hardship, but the town felt depressed, lacking in charm and atmosphere. The streets were wide. The shops were closed. The day was overcast. The people were absent. Our short overnight stay in Decazeville was a dismal experience, despite the comfortable hotel room we had booked.

While the town itself was forgettable, the look on the priest's face when we went to collect the second stamp in our credencials was really memorable. He was wearing a full-length black cassock, and a heavy silver cross hung from a long chain around his neck. He was young, and his face wore the keen smile of someone eager to help travelers along the Way. He asked the two standard questions that by then we knew by heart: "Where have you come from?" and "Where are going?" I answered both questions truthfully: "Rodez airport." The young priest, detecting a foreign accent and probably thinking I had not understood the question, tried again. When I augmented my initial response with my best smile and Richard said nothing to contradict me, he made no further inquiries. He stamped the pilgrim passport, smoothed his hair back from his forehead, cleared his throat, and wished us well. I imagined him thinking as he turned his back to us, *It takes all kinds . . .*

It is true that when looked at from the outside on that spring day in the year 2000, our pilgrimage did resemble more of a weekend jaunt than a serious attempt to walk the Way.

Then we did something that was unplanned. We slid our walking sticks under a large bush in the church grounds.

Mine was a fine-looking stick of solid wood with "Jungfrau" (not exactly local!) carved into its handle. I had seen it on display outside a tourist shop in a village somewhere during the last four days and had purchased it because it matched my hat, was comfortable to handle, and quite frankly just looked really pro. I liked it. Richard had simply stripped down a branch of a tree that he had found in a stream between Marcillac and Conques. That was Richard: not overly concerned with appearances. An aristocratic surname seemed to be all the credential needed, and even that he avoided displaying.

The *besace* (backpack) and *bourdon* (walking stick) are the two visible items by which a pilgrim may be identified. They are the external signs of someone who has agreed to travel in simplicity, unencumbered by social obligation; someone who has placed the intangible at the heart of her quest. What you cannot carry you do not take. The pilgrim's manual in which all this is noted doesn't actually mention the importance of color coordination, of course: my stick matched my hat. Neither does it mention that the stick, while symbolic, provides very real support over rough terrain. Not only that, it is a valuable asset when facing threatening dogs with very wide territories to guard.

Guidebooks warn about ferocious dogs in Spain but fail to describe the wild dogs that roam the French countryside. I met more than one snarling, slobbering, teeth-gnashing canine, walking through villages and over farmland in France. They provoked terror in me. I had to learn to stand my ground while hitting the ground several times with my stick and otherwise standing stock-still. I would glare fiercely at the hound and roar, "I shall pass!" It was far less impressive than Gandalf's famous cry in Peter Jackson's *Lord of the Rings*, "You shall not pass!" Even so, it did work. In each case, the beast was cowed enough not to advance any farther toward me.

I never failed to feel weak in the knees and out of breath after one of these encounters. Dogs that growl and bare their teeth truly do frighten me.

When I was a kid, maybe ten or so, I was cycling home from school one day along the riverbank when the next-door neighbor's dog started running alongside my bike and barking furiously. I didn't like the dog to start with and couldn't read the signals, so I just pedaled faster and started sticking out my right foot to scare him away. The more I did that, the more he barked and the faster he ran. The more he ran and the more he barked, the more excited he got. The more excited he got, the more frightened I got. I panicked. The dog bit me. I arrived home with a gash in my leg. Since it was the neighbor's dog, no one thought to check for rabies. I have never enjoyed being in the company of dogs. I find them unpredictable.

Are there any "rabid dogs" in your life that you need to keep at bay?

After we had slid our sticks side-by-side, deep under that bush, I said a silent prayer that we would find them there when we returned to the Way that summer. I was both philosophical and pragmatic: "Que sera, sera," and "I can always buy another one that matches my hat just as well." I didn't know if Richard attached any sentimental value to his riverbed find, but

I was pretty sure he was thinking, *We won't be able to take them on board with us on our flight back to Paris anyway.*

We left the church grounds, looked around for a taxi, and said goodbye to Decazeville. Our taxi driver said little as we sped the twenty minutes along the highway, back to the same airport we had left on foot four days previously. I felt disinclined to speak. I was overwhelmed by the sheer speed at which we were traveling. I like driving fast but don't like being driven fast. I don't like feeling that my well-being and safety are at someone else's mercy.

I consoled myself by repeating my own personal taxi mantras: "He loves his life, he needs his job—he loves his job, he needs his life." It helped. The airport had not changed in four days. The breakneck speed at which we'd returned to it shook my nervous system back into urban survival mode. The taxi ride prepared us for reentry into airspace and city touchdown.

Paris hadn't changed, either, in our absence. We had, though—just a little. Not so as you would notice, really.

My boots had changed just a little as well and were in need of some animal-fat treatment.

I dived into delivering more seminars, to which I now added the tale of our first four days of walking the Way of Saint James as a metaphor for a learning process.

Richard started planning the next phase of the pilgrimage that we would embark on in the summer.

PART 2   FRANCE
2000
SUMMER & AUTUMN
HALTE SUR LE CHEMIN
DE COMPOSTELLE
Montcuq

Mad Dogs and Englishmen—and Sometimes Pilgrims—Go Out in the Midday Sun!

In late July we took a night train from Paris to Rodez and then a local commuter train back to Decazeville. Our boots were slightly more scuffed and our backpacks not quite as spruce as they had been back in April.

After our Easter exploit, we thought we were seasoned enough walkers to take on ten more days in the full heat of summer. We were feeling confident as we headed back to the church grounds to collect our *bourdons*. The spot was easy to recognize: we had selected the biggest and bushiest bush closest to the church. It was exciting to anticipate being reunited with them. On the one hand, I didn't really expect to find them still lying there after a full three months in all kinds of weather. I told myself that some well-meaning gardener would have found them and put them to good use elsewhere — well, mine, at least! On the other hand, I didn't really know. I just hoped!

And then we saw them! Exactly as we had left them: side-by-side, tucked away in the undergrowth. They were unblemished and still ramrod straight. "So much for the quality of gardening in the church grounds," I muttered, smiling gratefully to myself. It was an extraordinary moment when we pulled them out intact from their hiding place and stamped the ground with their points, as if testing to see if they had kept their strength for us. It felt like a small miracle to me. A sign. A blessing. Even my inner critic, which likes to keep me on an even keel, feet to the ground, and resolutely pragmatic, only whispered, *It's just a stick, you know.*

**What small miracles have
you noticed taking place in
your life?**

I was overjoyed. Richard, as in all things, expressed a moderate amount of pleasure and promptly set to checking the map for the way out of town and the track up the mountain to our first night's stop, on farmland in Livinhac-le-Haut, on this second leg of the journey to Santiago.

Our accommodations were rudimentary: a single bed, a shower cubicle, and a stove over which we could heat the add-water-to-dry-pack dinner we had carted up the mountain with us. We moved on the next day to a three-course meal in a marketplace in the old town of Figeac. These changes of fortune, which Richard had willingly chosen, marked our ten days. (I was still a bit of a hanger-on where the planning was concerned.)

There was just one small event that took place on that first night, however, that I have not forgotten. The event troubled me then, and I am still not sure to this day how to interpret it with certainty.

Standing in the tiny space of the shower, water pouring over me, the mala I was wearing around my neck broke, its fifty-four tiny sandalwood meditation beads scattering everywhere. I frantically scrambled to catch them all in my hands before they went down the drain.

A mala is like a rosary. It is used to count repetitions of a mantra (a Sanskrit prayer with specific sound qualities and meaning), each bead representing one repetition. A mala has either fifty-four or 108 beads. I had proven to myself over time that the silent or vocal repetition of a mantra 108 times was an excellent way to clear the mind and develop the concentration necessary for effective meditation.

My mala had been given to me by Swami Veetamohananda, president of the Ramakrishna Vedantic Center in Gretz-Armainvilliers, France, on the morning he initiated me into my next step along the path of yoga. He would be my spiritual guide from the moment of my initiation ceremony onward.

I remember the morning well. It was a fine day in early April 1995. The sun had not yet risen. I skipped along the woodland path to the chapel where the ceremony would take place. I felt deliriously happy. I could see the waxing moon between the trees. The air was crisp. I sang to myself, "I've got the sun and the moon and the stars in my eyes"—over and over again until I reached the front steps of the big house, pushed open the enormous doors of the country mansion that had become an ashram for the order of the monks of Ramakrishna, slipped along a corridor, took my shoes off and slid quietly into the chapel. It was an auspicious moment in my life. I received my personal mantra, which would create an eternal link between me and my teacher, Swamiji, a relationship that I would come to understand as an expression of the holy bond between wo(man) and God.

So I was distraught when my mala broke in the shower that evening at the Communale Ferme Equestre in Livinhac-le-Haut. Once I had the precious beads in the palms of my wet hands, I searched for something to keep them safe in over the next ten days. I found a little cloth bag I had been using to carry my eating utensils. No beads had been lost, but I wondered what the broken mala might mean. Was it okay to be a practicing yogi and walk a Christian path? I didn't know.

A few years later, I walked away from my relationship with Swamiji. While his commitment to me, one whom he had accepted as his "disciple," would not break, I kept my distance from him for five years. I would keenly feel the loss of the close bond I had enjoyed with him, but what would emerge from the wreckage was a more mature, less starry-eyed relationship. My love for him would continue to deepen and expand over the years until his passing in November 2019.

Was the snapping of my first mala a harbinger of that later event? I couldn't say for sure. I still have the beads in their little bag. Swamiji would eventually give me a more beautiful mala, its thread much stronger than the original. He would also gently chastise me for wearing the new mala ostentatiously around my neck as a piece of jewelry. I have since never taken it out in public. I took his words to heart—always.

From Livinhac-le-Haut to Figeac, and on to Gréalou . . .

I remember the pure pleasure of squatting at the side of the road, basking in the morning sun, sipping tea from my thermos, and idling away the time. I don't remember the name of the village, but it was after Gréalou. We were heading for Limogne-en-Quercy. I remember the delicious feeling of there being no need to do anything or be anywhere . . . until the tea was finished. And then there was a need to move on toward the room we had booked for the night; but to get there, we had to face Les Causses du Quercy.

We set off reluctantly. It was already midday: the sun at its highest, many more kilometers in front of us and all of them up. Not only up but also over white limestone rock, which was unsupportive of tree roots. We were moving up and over Les Causses. Our path was well worn and wide, so those trees that had made a home for themselves on the outskirts of the rock face offered little in the way of shade.

We moved slowly under a relentless blue sky and the pounding rays of the sun. Sweat poured off me. The reverberating heat and the unforgiving hardness of the rock underfoot provoked a kind of delirium, a trudging madness,

on and up,

and on and up,

and on again.

What stopped me from tossing in the towel? Two things: 1) pilgrims walked, and 2) there was no choice.

And so we walked. Well, I slogged and trudged and groaned. I set my mind to dreaming up cool showers and ice-cold plunge pools. I transported myself to refrigerated sheets laid out on the evening's bed. I filled an imaginary freezer with different flavored fruit ice blocks and then opened the door and stood basking in their icy freshness, sucking on an orange one. I was *willing* my mind to soothe my aching, overheated body.

How does your mind help you overcome an obstacle of your own making?

When we finally arrived in the center of Limogne-en-Quercy, village residents were sitting leisurely in the local café, sipping their evening Pastis and watching life pass by. People spoke to each other rather than to their smartphones back in the year 2000. There were also still public telephone boxes that actually worked. You just needed the right size coins. We staggered, hot, exhausted, and aching all over, to the telephone box, conveniently situated in the center of the village and just over the road from the café. We called our evening hosts.

Then I had one of those I-am-going-to-die-right-here moments that would also become part of the journey to the tomb of Saint James. It was an instinctive response to the voice on the other end of the line that had cheerily welcomed our call with a "You'll find us just a couple of kilometers farther up the road."

Just a couple of kilometers up the road.

Just a couple of kilometers up the road!

The words seemed like a death knell. My body was screaming for transport. I had tears of despair in my eyes. I was afraid to sit down among the washed and suntanned bodies in the café in case the muscles in my legs seized up. I was desperate to just be at our lodgings, and the idea of a couple kilometers more was abhorrent. I was furious at the insensitivity of our hosts. I grumbled about the motorized species we had become, while desperately wanting to be motored to our room. I blamed Richard for choosing a place "so far out of town." I carefully did not acknowledge that planes and trains also belonged to our motorized species, and that without them, we would never have been able to undertake such an adventure.

And so, moaning and in pain, I gritted my teeth and walked those couple more kilometers up the road.

Our hosts were delightful, and I liked the sky-blue color of the window shutters on our *chambre d'hôte*.

Think of a time when your body was in extreme pain or a state of exhaustion. What strategies did you use to manage your condition?

What did you learn from the experience?

Moments of Grace

The convent in Vaylats was our first experience of an authentic Catholic institution: a place of worship that offered weary pilgrims a resting place for the night. Run by sisters, the convent was a haven of austere comfort where even our whispers echoed in the resounding silence. A statue of the Christ child with beckoning finger stood at the entrance to the dining room. I was drawn irresistibly to this little boy whose sweet demeanor graced the sisters' mealtimes.

The vegetable garden was well cared for and provided ample, healthy produce for evening meals. The little graveyard, with equal mounds of earth for each sister buried there, restored the word "humility" to its original Latin root, *humilis* (lowly, humble), literally meaning "on the ground," from *humus* (earth).

There was a thunderstorm brewing that evening. The sky hung, waiting and dark; the air was heavy, sticky, and crackling. I wandered down a long stretch of lawn to where a rose garden circled a lovely rotunda. In the center of the rotunda, Christ, with head tilted gently to one side, arms outstretched, welcomed the weary, the unloved, the forgotten, the ignorant, the sick, and the lonely to gaze upon his likeness and feel loved, remembered, recognized, and befriended.

Ever since I was a very young girl walking home on dark winter nights on my own, I had prayed to Jesus, my friend, to protect me.

It was a two-block walk from the Methodist church where I attended Sunday school and, later, Bible class. A straight walk up a well-lit Shirley Road, a left turn onto a poorly lit Ajax Street, and then left again at the bottom of Ajax into Achilles, also halfheartedly lit, thence to number 20, where my family lived.

My best friend's sister told me about a friend of hers who had been followed after leaving the church grounds. The man was breathing down her neck when she suddenly stopped short, whipped around to meet him face-to-face, and said sweetly but firmly, "Would you like to pray with me?" Sidelined by his victim's sheer bravado, the stalker disappeared swiftly into the night.

I never forgot the story and prayed that I, too,

would have the courage and forethought to act to save myself from whatever dangers might be lurking on the poorly lit streets of my childhood.

I was tested only once, but rather than confront whomever was following me, I knocked on a neighbor's door and asked to wait until I felt safe enough to continue on my way home.

I suppose other people had good luck charms, talismans, or some other form of self-care they used to combat fear and survive their childhoods. Mine was Jesus.

What was your antidote to fear when you were growing up?

Long after the thunderstorm that night, and long after we had moved on to other places and faces, the image of a young nun sitting quietly on a garden bench remains etched in my mind. Her contemplation of Christ in His own quiet acquiescence was interrupted by something I murmured. She showed me the beauty and nature of quiet time at the end of the day after work and before sleep; how to ease into the best of oneself by gazing upon an expression of the divine. Contemplation.

Meditation. Both impact the central nervous system and contribute to a sense of well-being.

The self that fragments over the course of an ordinary day slides graciously back into wholeness. A sense of completeness permeates the entire system, where all is included, whence all love flows.

Amen.

Butterflies, Cold Water, and a Cloister

Just outside Cahors, we stopped for the night at Chez Paulette. We indulged in the simple delight of Paulette's roasted chicken dinner served with fresh vegetables from her garden. Les poulets de Paulette was featured in guidebooks consulted by those walking the Way and did live up to its reputation. It came out of the oven glazed and golden. Each tender portion was copious, succulent, and dripping with the juice it had cooked in. The glass of cool, crisp white wine that came with the meal was sharp on the first sip, then fruity all the way down the rest of the glass. We shared the meal with people whom we had never met before. Conversations tended to be about where we had come from and where we were going next and where to eat and what to watch out for.

Paulette was not only a great cook but also the keeper of the keys to a very small but beautifully preserved chapel in her village. She gave us the keys, and we enjoyed a private visit before we moved on. It was in pristine condition: dust-free polished brass, silver, and possibly gold ornamenting the altar, the blues and reds of the stained glass window to the east behind it illuminated by the rays of the early morning sun.

I remember the quiet, like the silence in the garden in Vaylats, the fullness of which "passeth all understanding." If one is sipping cool water from a deep well on a hot summer's day, why would one not wish to stay? What keeps us on the move? Time passing? The cycle of seasons? The rising and setting of the sun?

For us the sun had risen, and it was time to be on our way again.

We walked that very long day toward a hostel called Aube Nouvelle. New Dawn. That day stands out in my mind for three reasons: butterflies, pain, and a glass of water.

Around midday I was walking through a field of long grass. There was a slight breeze. Children shouted joyfully beyond my sightline. I came to a standstill midfield. Tiny, brightly colored butterflies fluttered around my bare legs, kissing them playfully with their wings. They gifted me their joy—their lightness of being. Time stood still long enough for me to enjoy the fullness of this summer offering.

Later, toward evening, nearing sunset, the soles of my feet felt lacerated by miniature knives hidden inside my boots. Imaginary boulders of varying sizes filled my backpack, slowly crushing my vertebrae. Richard, like a horse smelling the proximity of its stable, galloped ahead. I was on my own, inside a tattered body feeling beyond tired and sorry for my dilapidated self.

Time advanced as slowly as each excruciating step forward.

Just after sunset we arrived at the New Dawn. We were greeted at the door by a smiling innkeeper who held out a glass of water—an exceptional glass of cool, clear water. The sheer gratitude I felt for the kindness of this gesture brought a lump to my throat, jeopardizing my ability to actually swallow this priceless gift. I brought the glass up to my sun-cracked lips and took a tiny sip and then another. Time was suspended in a moment of exquisite simplicity.

I heard the inner whisper of the one who keeps me on an even keel, saying that I was no one special—that it was the rule of the house to offer water to weary travelers on arrival. And despite those scratchy little words, there was no denying the kindness and thoughtfulness of the gesture.

Tears still find their way to the surface when I remember this gracious greeting at the New Dawn. It was the only place in the whole of those four years and three seasons where we were greeted with a glass of water.

And water to the traveler is like gold to the businessman; stock options to a CEO; dividends to the shareholder. Water had not yet gained its place as a precious commodity on the stock market. It was still freely available, and its value as the source of life largely ignored by the wealthy Western society I was a part of.

My appreciation for that glass of water was amplified by the intensity of the experiences of the day: the fleeting visit of those beautiful little butterflies, the agony of putting one foot in front of the other, the despair at being left behind, and, finally, feeling overwhelmed by kindness. All those emotions were powerful enough to suspend or distort my awareness of time passing; to interrupt the banality of the commonplace; to transform the ordinary into the extraordinary. The drone of every-day life had the habit of keeping these things just out of range of consciousness. Maybe this was why people walked the Way of Saint James: to find water in an ocean of pain and banality.

We finished the summer of 2000 in Moissac

after ten days of walking. The architectural perfection of the cloisters at the famous medieval abbey soothed my sun-stung eyes and offered me a place to rest my weary walker's legs. I also enjoyed an unadulterated contemplation of the annual tourist invasion of France's historical loveliness.

I was just beginning to get a sense of the superior status of the pilgrim as opposed to that of the tourist or the holidaymaker. A tourist moves quickly from artifact to artifact, snapping pictures. A holidaymaker wanders from pillar to pillar, chatting idly with friends. But a pilgrim contemplates things in silence, and her boots are never clean.

I rather fancied myself a pilgrim. From the lofty heights of spiritual thought, I could glance down upon the narrow and shallow preoccupations of the holiday-makers and tourists. In short, I would have been the perfect spiritual snob had I not needed to pee and eat like everyone else! The calls of nature tended to keep me at the right height and on the right part of the general playing field.

Two years later, in 2002, by then into the serious business of finding a bed for the night in Spanish hostels, I would discover that there was such a thing as pilgrim snobbism. Pilgrims did actually rank themselves and others according to some unwritten standards. The hierarchy was based on the length of time on the road, the number of kilometers covered in a day, and one's age. The older you were and the longer you walked, the more you gained in rank.

I have never forgotten the indignation in the voice of an athletic-looking Frenchman who threw his bag down on the ground in disgust somewhere in the middle of northern Spain. He protested loudly that he had walked over forty kilometers that day. He found it outrageous that there was no bed for him. He complained that some people had cheated. Some people, he said, got a bed before he did because they had arrived so early at the hostel, having walked so few kilometers in the day, or, worse, they had cycled! He ranted about being fed up with frauds and liars. He still accepted a mattress on the floor, and half the Spanish-speaking population didn't understand him anyway. It was obvious that he was operating according to one set of rules and that everyone else heeded another set. I wondered whether he fumed all the way to Santiago, or whether the journey eventually whittled away his discontent.

Learning the subtle rites and rules of conduct of the pilgrim was something we would do two years later, when we walked across northern Spain. But in Moissac in the summer of 2000, I was just beginning to feel the smug satisfaction of my newfound status as pilgrim-on-the-road-to-Santiago. I quite enjoyed the role at sites like the cloisters in Moissac. I felt part of the medieval pageant and pretended not to notice if a tourist snapped a picture of me as one of the figures in the tableau.

But that was what one part of me was doing. Another part of me, totally unaware of the presence of others, stood in wonder before a small statue of the Virgin. She is called Our Lady of Solitude. She sits, head to one side, a loosely wrapped cloak covering her head and body. You can make out her spread knees beneath the cloak. They appear to be set in the posture of meditation: *padmasana*, the lotus pose. Her face wears a mournful expression and her eyes are cast downward—closed, perhaps. To see her is to feel her loneliness and her grief at the loss of her beloved son to his chosen path.

What moments of grace, of grief, of loneliness, has life granted you?

Which of these moments has been your greatest teacher?

We left the Way in Moissac and caught a train back to Paris. We took our sticks with us this time.

The Mellow Season

At the end of October 2000, true to our vow to set out from wherever we had left off, we took another high-speed train from Paris to Agen, then a regional train back to Moissac. While the trimmings were the same—chic leather hat, worn leather boots, scuffed backpack, scratched wooden walking stick—we now carried extra layers of merino wool clothing for the cooler nights and waterproofs for the backpacks and our bodies. It was a welcome break from the city, and I was looking forward to it.

We had by then collected twelve stamps in the credencial, and we felt quite comfortable with a walking rhythm of roughly twenty-five kilometers per day. The Way was well signposted, and we already knew parts of the landscape from the many holidays we had enjoyed in the region. The walking was relatively easy, over undulating farmland through little villages and past hospitable dogs. It didn't rain once, and I only needed my extra layers starting out in the mornings and finishing at the end of each day. We were well equipped.

I liked walking through the mellow tones of late October/early November in France. The grapes had been harvested, leaving mottled red-and-yellow leaves drooping in their place. We tramped and swished through rusting leaves fallen from the tall plane trees lining our pathway. I felt the sharper notes of winter in the shortened days and crisp sunrises. It was the season of decay and absence, of burning detritus and black-birds etched against startlingly blue skies. Nature was preparing for hibernation. Farmers were plowing the earth for next year's planting. The trees in the orchards were bare—much of their fruit had fallen and lay in the wet grass at the foot of the trunks.

One afternoon we sat on a fallen tree trunk, resting while we munched on a couple of apples that had fallen too late for the harvest.

It was my season for poetic melancholy:

Earth churned,
and chunked
to lie fallow.
Trees stripped

and stark on blue
skies chilled and filled
with smells of fruit,
rotting sweetly in wet
grass, emerald, beneath
soggy leftover leaves.

The hostels we stopped in each night were empty and eerie. I don't remember their names, but one was an old castle that had been converted to accommodate pilgrims. It was perched on a hillside, and some of its outer walls were crumbling. We felt like intruders on a scene set for a Hitchcock thriller. We whispered to each other, afraid to disturb the spooky silence. Despite an embarrassing number of beds to choose from, that night in the communal dormitory, we huddled together on one narrow bed inside our separate sleeping bags. In fact, it was a lonely experience being the only ones on the road.

We met no one else, except on the night we booked a room in a country house near Miradoux. The hosts were a handsome couple, wealthy and worldly. We were invited to engage with their other guests (they happened to be nonwalkers) in conversations that felt more like a competition and covered a variety of subjects: politics under Jacques Chirac, France in the twenty-first century, and a few contemporary authors. I held my own on the weather and could count on my New Zealand birth to earn me easy points in the quaint-people-I-have-met stakes.

I really dislike that kind of evening. I am a competitor but hate it when I am losing due to what I deem unfair competition. When I am winning, however, I prefer to nobly resist flaunting it—provided it's obvious to everyone present who's winning. I don't admire either of these two facets of my personality, and I work on them—from time to time . . .

That evening brought back some painful memories of the slow acculturation process I underwent having decided to make France my home back in 1980. There was a time, about six months into what felt like a life sentence, when the charm of being a long-term tourist in Paris wore off. I didn't speak French well enough to hold my own in a conversation back in the early eighties. The rules of conversation were totally different from those of my Anglo-Saxon heritage. French people do not, as a rule, ask questions at dinner parties, not wishing to intrude on personal territory and therefore appear rude. One has to talk fast, with panache, and know how to hold the floor in a conversation. The point is not to include others but to seduce them with the brilliance of your discourse or insider knowledge. Stopping to fill your lungs with air is an error that you pay for by having the floor whipped from under your feet. The verbal jousting sets off in another direction, led by a new knight in dazzling style.

It has been a long, hard road from that beginning to delivering training courses in French and making the asking of questions my legitimate profession: coaching.

Share an experience of a dinner party when you were the outsider.

Did you do anything to get yourself included?

How do you enjoy the role of bystander on social occasions?

We kept moving. After Miradoux came Lectoure and then La Romieu, and somewhere Marsolan and then Condom, our destination, where we first spotted the Pyrenees.

I can still see Richard's joyful face and hear the delight in his voice when he announced grandly: "The Pyrenees." He could have been introducing me to royalty, and I almost curtsied. "Sire" not far from my lips. He didn't often do the aristocratic number that his particule and historical lineage allowed him. What I could see in the haze-free sky was a tiny row of white peaks far away in the distance. "The Pyrenees," he repeated, as if reciting a mantra inherited from his paternal grandmother, an eccentric but youthful old lady who chose to end her days in a hotel at the foot of these same mountains. I imagined her standing in awe before their majesty. "The Pyrenees!" she would have iterated on a daily basis. She may also have been a little mad. From where we were standing, they looked like foothills to me, but I tried to rise to the occasion and not scoff at Richard's enthusiasm.

"Gosh, yes, the Pyrenees!" I echoed, straining to sound suitably impressed. I would dispel all disparaging thoughts about the "foothills" two summers hence when we crossed them to get into Spain. They were indeed mountains that commanded respect from all on foot.

Five days was enough to get the full flavor of autumn and its melancholy. We had no intention of walking in winter. Our venture had begun in spring, had developed in summer, and had been tested in autumn. Imagining barren landscapes, short days, and empty, unheated hostels was enough to deter me from ever wanting to walk the Way in winter.

We stayed overnight in Condom in a nice motel with an outdoor swimming pool, closed for the winter. I knew I would enjoy starting a new leg of the journey with a thirty-minute, early morning swim the following summer in that pool.

We took the first train back to Paris the following morning to resume life as if nothing had changed. The Way was beginning to work small changes within us, but we were the only ones to notice them. We paid more attention to the different moods of the sky and the way some birds would perch a little longer on our balcony before flitting off.

PART 3   FRANCE
Sur les chemins de St-Jacques
OFFICE
DE TOURISME
MONTREAL-DU-GERS
2001   SUMMER

Empty Mind—
Full Backpack

When we set out from Condom on August 10, 2001, moving through the Gers to the Basque Country and finally to the foot of the mountain pass that would lead us to Spain, we belonged to one world. When we left the path on August 22, it would take us only twenty days to get to September 11, when we would irrevocably belong to another one. The secure and tranquil world I thought I had grown up in was on the verge of another era that summer, but I was blissfully unaware of what was brewing.

Planes crashing into the Twin Towers in New York, madmen gunning down an entire editorial staff of a French magazine in Paris, trucks driving head-on into festive July 14 crowds in Nice, a lone gunman in

Norway, shooting kids on a holiday island, devastating swings in climate, and pandemics were not part of the world we inhabited in August of 2001.

On the Camino that summer, the only news of any real interest was the weather forecast, but even that couldn't compete with the evening reports on blisters, sprains, and torn ligaments shared among walkers and pilgrims alike.

The walking we were doing every day, up hill and down dale, kilometer after kilometer, was, in hindsight, whittling away at the superfluous and the extraneous. I got closer to my essential self as my boots got muddier and my clothes more worn. The Way was strengthening my body and clearing my mind, equipping me to deal with a post-9/11 world.

> ## In hindsight, did anything you were doing prepare you for a post-9/11 world?

My mind may have emptied itself of excess baggage over those twelve days of summer, but my backpack did not! I remained firmly attached to my morning cup of tea. This meant carrying not only cold water in a CamelBak for regular sipping but also a thermos of boiling water for my morning "péché mignon". The intense pleasure of sipping hot tea in the morning sunshine, lounging on a park bench or against the rim of a village fountain, far outweighed the inconvenience of carrying an extra kilo or two. I applied the same reasoning to the face and body creams I carried all the way to Santiago: the pleasure outweighed the inconvenience. That didn't stop me questioning my "addiction" every morning, when I hoisted my backpack onto my shoulders, groaning under the additional weight. But I never doubted my "wisdom" come midmorning. I celebrated Nivea cream post-shower. I may have cursed the extra weight, but I never regretted the two moments of daily pleasure, considering them as essential as the sleeping bag and the sun hat. So, the body strengthened, the mind emptied, and the bag stayed full. And that's just how it was.

Are you carrying extra weight?

What pleasure does it bring you?

The Camino worked on everyone differently. I met a woman who was walking to assuage the devastating loss of her daughter to cancer. Another told me she was walking to substitute debilitating feelings of guilt and shame with a more acceptable version of pain—one that she could massage in the evening. A few people I came across were, I guess, walking to escape boredom: to find companionship and sex, although they never mentioned the latter. I overheard a few talking about the walk as a religious experience, although they never discussed it with me directly.

I was called irresistibly back to this path once I had had my first taste of it. The easiest explanation is that I like to complete what has been started. I like to pick up a pen and close the unfinished circle on a page even if someone else has drawn the first arc.

Often what people initially thought they were walking to Santiago for was not what they found along the Way. The person who set out was not the same as the one who arrived. I would be able to state this personally and with certitude much later.

But now it was the height of summer. We were in the southwest of France. The sheer beauty of the countryside, with its carefully tended villages and towns, made even the toughest days worthwhile.

Small Places— Big Learning

Montréal-du-Gers

It was August 10. There was a chap standing in the doorway of our hostel in Montréal-du-Gers. He was wearing shiny blue Lycra Bermudas with a matching tight-fitting tank top zipped up over a pot belly. Neat little red shoes sat at the bottom of a pair of hairy legs. He was smiling and looking quite refreshed for someone, like us, at the end of a day's walking.

I asked the standard question: "How many kilometers have you done today?"

"Only seventy-eight," he replied, grinning ruefully.

I gaped. I was still trying to get my head around

the fact that someone could walk seventy-eight kilometers in a day when he pointed to his bike. I giggled and let my breath go. I didn't need to voice my incredulity; it was written all over my face and covered a wide spectrum of emotions: utter despair (we had only managed twenty-five kilometers), dumbfounded admiration (for a superhero in blue Lycra), contempt (for a second-rate pilgrim with hairy legs on a bicycle).

It was the first time I actually realized that there were people cycling to Santiago, following a path not unlike that of the walkers. I put cyclists in the same category as those who hired firms to carry their bags from one night's accommodation to the next. Taking the fast and easy route felt to me like cheating. I was a bit uppity about cyclists sharing the same hostels as pilgrims, who could only be considered genuine if they were on foot. I don't know who or what gave me the right to judge anyone else, but I did. It was all part of that me who was moving toward Santiago twenty years ago.

> **What kind of world did you live in
> twenty years ago?**
>
> **What kind of eyes did you judge
> the world with back then?**

From Montréal-du-Gers we moved on to Eauze and Nogaro, then Lanne-Soubiran, arriving in Aire on the river Adour on August 14.

Aire-sur-l'Adour

The cool morning air warmed steadily until the ferocious midday sun sapped our energy to the point where eating our longed-for picnic sandwiches felt almost like too much hard work. After lunch, Richard and I stretched out in a field down by the river, our heads resting on our backpacks. I held my stick close in case I spotted the green-and-yellow of an indolent grass snake slithering too close for comfort. Insects hummed, buzzed, and chirped a lazy serenade to our prostrate selves. The air pinned us to the ground and my eyes slowly closed.

Until, striding, heads down, wearing hikers' kits,

a man and a woman appeared at the top of the field. They talked loudly as they propelled themselves forward down the field and across the space in front of us, surging onward with the aid of two walking poles each. They looked like they meant business! I heard their vowel sounds as Canadian and expected them to stop and share a few words with us, but they were too intent on their own conversation and their determined thrust forward. I was staggered (as far as I could be, given my prone position) by the speed with which they were covering ground. I called out, but they didn't hear; they were going too fast.

We met them later in another hostel and got chatting in the communal area where everyone made their evening meal. We spoke the same language, so there was natural gravitation between us. They told us they had limited time available, a huge distance to cover, and a plane to catch at the end of it. I did not feel envious of them, but I did learn one important thing from them: two poles are better than one!

Later, near a prehistoric archaeological site in Spain, I met a Brazilian chap who was limping along, desperately trying to catch up with his friends. They had left him behind with his tendinitis because they also had to catch a plane. He said he accepted his friends' decision. It seemed unfair to me, but maybe that was the deal they had made together. We had made a different one: stop if you can't go any farther and return home. I guessed he would miss his flight back home, and who knows what that might have cost him.

Have you ever had a well thought-out plan that you had to let go of?

I felt privileged to live in France, where it was easy for us to come and go by bus or train. Tickets were cheap, and schedules could be changed for little extra cost. Both the streaking Canadian couple and the limping Brazilian taught me to avoid ever letting the financial pressure of a return ticket dictate the terms of our journey. The Way was too full of surprises and un-predictable events to want to be held hostage to a prior travel arrangement.

On the whole, a pilgrimage has its own schedule. It determines you, not the other way around. Even the most well thought-out plans could be thwarted by the unexpected.

To a certain extent we ourselves were held hostage to a professional schedule. Walking summers over longish periods post-2000, we could still be back in Paris in time to honor our fall obligations. We never had, or never made, enough time to walk the whole of the Way in one go.

> ## In what way does your profession restrict your freedom? Set you free?

Cold Turkey

Navarrenx

We walked into Navarrenx on August 19. The previous four days had gone according to plan, or at least without anything of note having happened. In Navarrenx, though, something did happen—something that could not have been foreseen. While the event in itself is a tiny thing, it left its mark on me.

I absolutely do not remember how I came to be standing outside a church, face-to-face with a Catholic priest.

He holds my hand and my gaze a fraction longer than is strictly necessary for a first encounter. His eyes look deeply into mine. He whispers softly, "Ultreia." I know the meaning of the word. He is sending me forward and onward with the famous cry of the pilgrim on her way to Santiago.

Except this is no cry. It is soft and sweet and seductive but, curiously enough, not sexual. It is not an invitation to indulge in a sexual fantasy, but his voice nevertheless caresses my ear.

His energy field is irresistible. It pulls me toward it like a helpless moth to the evening light.

Suddenly, as if plugged into an electric socket, my whole body is charged with electricity.

I light up! I beam! I want to dance! I feel I could run all the way to Santiago—and back!

The fatigue that has been accumulating in my mind and legs after endless hours and days of walking just up and disappears.

I feel in love with the world and generous toward all its creatures. Magic is in the air. I am as high as a kite through natural means.

I wish I could remember what else he said to me. All I have kept of this extraordinary exchange is an overriding sense of having met a kindred spirit on the way to a holy shrine.

No, it wasn't a Damascus moment.

Because.

The following day I crashed. If I had been a drinker,

I would have described the sensation as a massive hangover. I was out of sorts the whole day. My feet were leaden. I had to sit down a lot. I sighed as I walked. Each step forward was a major effort. *Ultreia* was just a fancy formula: a trinket to collect along the Way to Santiago.

Even today I find it hard to believe that a priest could induce the state of ecstasy I very clearly experienced, or that I could have felt so dreadful the following day.

Something vaguely similar happened when I consumed a bar of chocolate in haste in the middle of a squash competition. I was losing and was desperate for an energy boost. The only thing available was a chocolate bar. The sugar rushed into my bloodstream, propelling my legs and arms to make some dazzling shots. My brilliant performance lasted less than a game. The quick fix wore off and my body could no longer respond to my opponent's onslaught. I was slaughtered for want of energy.

The contact with the priest in Navarrenx had nothing to do with chocolate bars. I could not explain the soaring energy in me any more than I could explain the radical plummet the following day. I put it down to "mysterious occurrences" experienced by those who walked the Way.

I did hear the following year that the priest in question no longer held his post at the church in Navarrenx. It was just a routine change of diocese, apparently. Or was it?

What I do know today is that regular spiritual practice builds a strong psyche. A powerful psyche can charm and disarm. It can dress itself in coats of many colors. It can seduce even its owner. Someone caught in her own spiritual superiority does little to advance the cause of human kindness. I don't know what the antidote might be, but I am sure it is not chocolate.

Looking back on my encounter in Navarrenx, I wonder if "my" priest had been seduced by his own power. Had local church authorities had him removed because they considered him a risk to gullible pilgrims like me? Had he been perceived as a threat to less talented priests?

> **Have you ever experienced an inexplicable, overwhelming joy?**
>
> **How long did the feeling last, and what happened afterward?**

Taken for a Ride

The Basque Country

We were among the last of the day's guests to arrive at the farmyard in Aroue, some twenty kilometers farther on from the priest in Navarrenx. We felt tired and were looking forward to lodgings with a difference. Word of mouth had it that this place was worth a stop, and guidebooks, too, would later claim it served up an authentic taste of the Basque Country. We were close to the gateway to Spain by then, and the roads were starting to converge. Pilgrims, travelers, walkers, and wanderers were more numerous, and the choice of accommodations more limited. The farmhouse was an obvious pick.

We were greeted by snorting, squealing pigs, mewling kittens, squawking chickens, lounging dogs, and skulking cats. A grinning donkey posed next to a silent horse, muddy cows shambled around a trough of animal feed, and food scraps were scattered indiscriminately across the yard. The only thing missing from the farmyard tableau was someone singing "Old MacDonald." I was not charmed. We picked our way across the ragged, muddy yard, careful not to upset the rural decor. I kept a close eye on the lounging dogs, whose docility I didn't fully trust. My stick remained firmly on guard duty.

We entered the two-story farmhouse and climbed the stairs to our room for the night. There was nothing wrong or memorable about the room. The corridor was filled with the amicable chatter of tired walkers waiting patiently to take their turn in the bathroom. I could hear people bustling around in the kitchen, clanging pots and pans, and the smell of our evening meal wafted up the stairway. I took a guess: poulet basquaise. Everything looked and smelled authentic, but none of it rang true to me. There was something orchestrated about the rural scene outside that made me feel like an unwilling actress in someone else's play. The place obviously wasn't what it was cracked up to be: "an authentic farm-stay in the Basque Country." It was only for one night, and no one was forcing us to stay, but still I felt I was being taken for a ride.

Sham or not, we were part of an eager buzz of pilgrims converging on this farmhouse.

I was reminded of the many holy sites I had visited along the hippie trails in Southeast Asia in my twenties. There was always a keen bustle of pilgrims and tourists in and around the temple, and where there were visitors, there were vendors. They had their own pricing codes for Westerners, based on a sliding scale: from hippies doing Asia on a shoestring to tourists in air-conditioned taxis or buses. I was on a shoestring.

I can still see myself in my beads and sarong, long hair and sandals. I can hear feigned outrage in my voice as I haggle over a ring with a vendor in Bali, telling him that I am staying in a hut on Kuta Beach and not in some fancy hotel in Sanur. I can see myself walking away, a strut in my stride, bearing the ring for a price that satisfied my pride and left money in my pocket. Both vendor and buyer were happy with the outcome of the game.

Thirty years later, I am in shorts and drip-dry shirt; my hair is much shorter, and I am wearing walking boots. I pride myself on being travel-savvy, and what I am being offered here is not the real deal. It is annoying but not humiliating.

Unlike the time I was sitting at a terrace café on the Left Bank in Paris with a friend and the waiter delivered my salad without a knife and fork. What happened next was not only annoying but also humiliating. I called the waiter back and indignantly demanded the cutlery. I was furious that he would treat me like a tourist when I was so eager to demonstrate how au fait I was with eating out in Paris. Had I not been so keen to impress my friend, my pride would not have taken such a blow when the waiter came back and elegantly plunked a soup spoon next to my plate. Had he added salt, it could not have stung more.

I had chosen the café because of its waiters dressed in the traditional garb of the garçon: black waistcoat and long white apron over black trousers. They glided and pirouetted from table to table, balancing glasses, filled or empty; plates piled high, filled or empty. The waiters and I were complicit in my attempt to show off to my friend, until the garçon delivered the fatal spoon instead of a knife and fork. I shouted in genuine fury— in French—that I was a local, not a tourist, and that no one, anywhere in the world, eats a bloody salad with a spoon. I wish I could have seen the very funny side of the scene, but my pride was wounded. My friend still teases me about it, and I still cringe.

On reflection, I wasn't really discontented with our night's lodgings, as such; rather, I was taken by a desire to let the owner know I thought he was out for a quick buck, and he wasn't fooling me with his authentic farm-yard nonsense. I wanted him to know I knew fake from real, but I was caught up in another desire: to be, and not just act, the humble pilgrim on her way to Santiago.

Pointing the finger at the owner was more about my own pride than about a need to expose a falsehood. I felt pretty certain that he was milking the Way for all it was worth: peddling squalor because he was too lazy to make an honest living off the land like actual Basque farmers. I thought he was a crafty businessman sitting on a little gold mine at the confluence of many paths at the foot of the mountain pass. He was lining his pocket without much effort. In fact, the less effort he made, the more genuine his farmyard mess looked. The more urban the pilgrim, the more enchanted he or she would be by the genuineness of the rural experience on display.

He was not unique. There were more like him on the other side of the mountain.

Have you ever been taken for a ride?

> How did that happen?
>
> How did the story end?

A Rooster behind Lace Curtains

Ostabat

The following morning we rose early, left the visitors' book unsigned, crossed the mud and slop of the yard for the last time and, without a single glance back, headed on toward Ostabat. Six hours later we met our new hosts for the evening. This time we had opted for *chambre d'hôte* accommodation. We were shown to a very clean and tidy room with attached bathroom. There were lace curtains on the windows and a matching bedcover neatly tucked over a double bed. It was a room of soft tastes and colors, enveloping and warm. It was lovely to look at but difficult not to feel like we were messing up the decor with the grime of the day still clinging to us.

We showered and did our best to stack the contents of our backpacks in neat piles under one of the window ledges. Our hosts for the evening were a couple of Basque-speaking retirees. Our dinner was, predictably, poulet basquaise, and unpredictably, ruined by the rooster!

It reminded me of winter mealtimes in Christchurch. I hated the ritual of cooked vegetables on the table by 5:00 p.m., when my father got home from work. But mostly I remember the adage "children should be seen and not heard," an injunction uttered by my father presumably whenever I opened my mouth to complain. Or maybe the five-mile bike ride home from the office in a freezing easterly wind left him with no patience to deal with the chatter of a child. I don't know how reliable my childhood memories are, but I do know that our host in Ostabat that night triggered in me the same silent black fury. I slipped back to an age when my mother's voice could admonish me for lack of gratitude. She would usually begin with: "When I was your age, I never had . . ." She would try to shake me out of my sulking bad temper by teasing me about my lower lip being so long that one day I would trip over it. Fury born of helplessness in the presence of the all-powerful.

While my five-year-old self was practicing voodoo rites on our domineering, self-opinionated, bigoted host, my mother's daughter smiled politely and ate everything put in front of her—with gratitude. It was the price of the meal and the clean comfort of "home."

The fact that Richard was writing for *L'Express*, one of France's major weeklies, made him attractive to our male host, who had a cause to promote and a culture to defend. The Basque Country has a unique history and language and has the luck or misfortune to be situated on both sides of the Spanish and French borders. For many years Basque terrorists plagued the Spanish government and the local population with bombs and shootings in an attempt to bring attention to their fight for independent rule of their territory. While culturally aligned to the cause, the French Basques had never displayed the same terrorist tactics. Spanish Basques were rich; the French Basques, poor. The social security system in France was better than that in Spain, so the fight had never had the same allure for the French Basques.

The host we engaged with was a Basque first and a Frenchman second. He was at home in the Basque Country but not in France. I could have shared notes on what it was like to feel like a foreigner in the land of one's choosing, but he couldn't tolerate foreigners, certainly not female ones.

His wife was incapable of wedging words into her husband's monologue, and she did not dare intervene in the dialogue conducted exclusively with "the journalist." We women were sidelined and too polite to complain. It was another form of being held hostage. In order to keep the real or imaginary balance of exchange, I accepted a bullying host.

And it was not the first time I had experienced being demeaned by a man in a social context. It is not a French specialty.

I had returned to New Zealand via Sydney to attend an intercultural conference as a guest speaker. On the evening after the conference, I was invited to a dinner party. I was entertaining the dozen or so people around the table with a few anecdotes from the conference and offering my opinion about cultural differences between the French and the Australians. I had been living in France for about ten years at the time.

The host interrupted me when I was in full flight to remark, in an Australian drawl as thick as a dog's turd, that I had not lost my Kiwi accent. It was a major putdown. It cut all further discussion and interest in what I had to say. It was as if everyone had needed to be reminded of the rules of polite dinner table conversation. I should have remembered that the code of conduct

Down Under when the sexes came together to eat was one of male-dominated banter.

The idea is that women are not skilled banterers, which means that the roles of listener, titterer, and part-time contributor tend to be what they excel at. I had stood out like a tall poppy, and it had been time to cut me down to size—the Australian way. It hurt me. It insulted me.

I was convinced no one could appreciate what a delight it was for me to be speaking in my own language about things that interested me and, clearly, others. I was sure no one could understand the terrible pain of acculturation I had experienced in my first few years in France after the glamour of being a tourist had worn off. I was certain no one understood, either, that French etiquette meant that whoever had something interesting to impart was listened to regardless of gender. I felt just as helpless and as misunderstood as I had as a five-year-old eating dinner at the family table. I seethed silent black fury!

Meanwhile, back at the Ostabat ranch with the rooster and his *poule*, Richard and I continued to experiment with the risks involved in staying with local people.

There was romance in slipping momentarily into someone's life, getting a glimpse of it, and then sliding away the following day. There was an unspoken contract that all parties unconsciously signed; it was in force for twenty-four hours or less. It was all, however, a little like Russian roulette.

That night in Ostabat I got the bullet in the head. No one died, but I did not see a way around the problem. Being a guest at someone else's table prevented me from expressing my thoughts and feelings for fear of being rude. The usual option open to women in these types of situations is to cluster together and start conversations that bypass the men, but our hostess that evening seemed content or condemned to serve the chicken with *pipérade* rather than engage in any conversation on the side with me. My silent black fury dwindled to sheer dull gray boredom, and I left the table without making any attempt at a smile.

In the space of two nights, we had been treated to a phony and then a domineering bigot. I made a quiet vow to avoid, where possible, signing this kind of contract elsewhere. I hoped the following night in Saint-Jean-Pied-de-Port would be nothing but clean and peaceful; that we would pay the price announced at the door; that there would be no hidden extras.

Have you ever been held hostage
at someone's dinner party?

How did you handle it?

An Achilles' Heel

Saint-Jean-Pied-de-Port

A six-hour walk the following day took us to Saint-Jean-Pied-de-Port, at the foot of the Pyrenees. The walk was beautiful and uneventful. It was the arrival at the portal to the medieval town that was exciting. The day was sunny and there were bubbles of people of all nationalities thronging the entrance to the town.

We stopped to savor the moment. I leaned against one of the portal's arches just to feel the coolness of the stone. I was thinking about the number of pilgrims who had passed through this gateway on their way over the mountains. Weary from the walk, I also felt a sense of awe at being part of a thousand years of history. I felt proud of what we had achieved so far and at the same time humbled by the insignificance of our place in the story of the Way.

While I was engaged in these musings, I looked up and noticed that people were taking photos of us. I felt a bit silly when I realized that we had been recognized as pilgrims. The cloth scallop shell dangling at the back of each of our backpacks was a dead giveaway, as were our clothes and, just possibly, our smell!

The people with the cameras were dressed like day-trippers, in shorts, T-shirts, and flip-flops. I stepped out of my daydreaming and into the part being offered me by their reverent glances and snapshots. I became the pilgrim they were imagining and smiled graciously, adjusting my pose and lolling—elegantly, I hoped— against the portal: a weary traveler taking time out from her pilgriming. I don't know what their cameras captured of this moment or what they were really thinking, but the photo that I have kept in my mind is of two people looking mightily pleased with themselves, surrounded by a group of gawping tourists.

We enjoyed a day in the old town just wandering without the weight of a backpack. Stalls of craftsmen selling their wares lined the main street. Apart from the clothes they were wearing, I could easily imagine that the scene hadn't changed much since the Middle Ages. Looking down to the end of the street, I could see the portal we had walked through and been photographed at the day before. Looking up the street, I could see the portal through which we would need to pass to begin our climb up toward the mountain pass.

I was enjoying wandering from stall to stall, admiring all sorts of handicrafts, most of which I could not carry on my back, when some beautifully hand-tooled leather goods caught my eye. I found a soft tan leather belt with a simple silver buckle. It was one knuckle wide and rolled easily around my wrist. Relatively thick and unadorned, it would last a lifetime, and I would be unlikely to hand it on to the secondhand shop. I could choose to either carry it or wear it immediately. I bought it without further thought.

It was the twenty-second of August, and this was the last leg for us that summer. We would pick up the trail here the following year. I had hoped to cross the border into Spain on this leg, but Richard was suffering from tendinitis, so I had to let go of my desire to keep going.

The longer I walked the Way, the more addictive it became. I had begun to crave my daily fix of endorphins, those amazing hormones that allow the brain to camouflage pain and substitute it with sensations of pleasure. I had crossed a threshold after which stopping seemed much worse than going on. On the other side of the threshold, however, tendinitis was a real risk.

After two weeks of walking between twenty-five and thirty kilometers a day, Richard's Achilles' tendon was on fire, and all I wanted was to shoot for another week of daily thirty-kilometer fixes. He had hobbled into Saint-Jean the day before, and I had thought that a day of rest and sightseeing would see him ready to move on again. Now I was champing at the bit to be on the move again, but Richard had to stop for a bit more.

I griped and fumed, but, short of continuing on my own, there was nothing to be done. We were in it together, and we had made a pact to stop when we could go no farther. I was really peeved and struggled to sympathize with his pain, convinced it was part of a broader plan to thwart my doing what I wanted to do: continue!

Looking back, after twenty years of personal development and an awareness of family systems and how personal loyalties leave their indelible imprint on all members of the group, I read my peevishness as a form of a then unconscious loyalty toward my mother. I had been showing her how to get what she wanted as far back as I can remember. And all without her ever having asked me to do so! Growing up, I was witness to the following pattern:

Mum says, "Let's do x."

Dad says no.

Mum asks, "Why not?"

Dad replies, "Because I don't want to!"

The words changed, but the pattern didn't. It invariably ended in my mother's disappointment and frustration, the clenching of my father's jaw, and a taut silence—until the next round.

I must have been quite young when I made the unconscious decision to take on my mother's plight as my own. My unformulated vow was, *I will realize all your dreams for you.*

There are many hidden facets to such a vow: fierce determination that brooks no opposition, a willingness to go it alone, a capacity to hide emotion, parsimonious sharing of self, a wariness of anyone who could thwart my plans—as well as a joyous relationship to life, love and friendship.

I first screamed consciously at my father—on my mother's behalf, though I didn't quite understand that that was what motivated me—when I was thirteen. I told my father after dinner one summer evening that I wanted to go to Australia with a junior athletic team.

He said no.

I hit the roof and shouted that I was going anyway.

He said very quietly, "And where are you going to get the money from?"

I roared that I would work every weekend.

I did.

I served ice cream every Sunday for a year and went to Australia at the end of it.

Over the years, whenever a no from a male partner threatened to thwart a personal desire, I learned to reduce the heat on the inner burner before a flaming rage engulfed me. I did learn that a no from a man was not necessarily life-threatening, and that the matter could be discussed and dealt with in an adult way.

And that is what happened in Saint-Jean-Pied-de-Port when Richard said we had to stop because he had Achilles tendinitis. I did not unconsciously take up my mother's crusade, but I did feel the heat build up around the no to our continuing over the mountain. I would let the flames engulf me entirely the following year.

> **What kind of family loyalty drives you to do things that are not in your own best interest.**

PART 4   FRANCE TO SPAIN
2002 SUMMER
BELORADO

Over the Mountain

A year had passed. It was summer again. I knew the pilgrimage was working its subtle magic on my soul, but I couldn't say with any certainty exactly what that magic was when we began our journey again, in August 2002. I had continued weaving amusing anecdotes about the first two years of walking the Camino into the opening sequence of each of my new coaching classes. The mental and physical effort the pilgrimage demanded was a perfect metaphor for the journey the trainees were undertaking. I asked them to think about previous learning journeys they had been on and to consider what was the same and what was different, as they listened to my tale. It was also an opportunity to familiarize themselves with the tones and rhythms of a New Zealand voice speaking French words. When I finished speaking, I asked them to share their own stories with the "stranger" next to them—the one they would be symbolically walking with for the duration of the class, the next seven months.

As we set out in the summer of 2002, ready to tackle the passage across the mountains, the pilgrimage felt to me like an adventure still begging to be completed. I was keen to get going. I like having targets, and I had learned early in life to set and achieve them. Roncesvalles, on the other side of the mountain, in Spain, was beckoning me.

It was August 15 when we walked back into Saint-Jean-Pied-de-Port. We had taken trains and buses from Paris to a small Basque Country town, Saint-Palais, where we had picked up the trail again. Our goal had been to loosen up the limbs and find our rhythm in preparation for the crossing of the Pyrenees. We had broken the thirty-kilometer distance between Saint-Palais and Saint-Jean into two parts, so we were not overly tired when, on the second night, we reached our hostel in Saint-Jean.

The day had been hot, but the air was finally beginning to cool. The little streets were just as noisy as they had been the year before, full of ambling tourists, colorful wares, and outdoor cafés. This time we did not wander from stall to stall, soaking up the holiday atmosphere. We were focused on what lay ahead for us the following day: the climb. We collected another stamp from the pilgrims' bureau, shopped at the local supermarket for our dinner that night and picnic the following day, unrolled our sleeping bags on two available bunks, showered, snacked, and turned the lights out not long after dark.

The following morning, the dawn silence was broken by the sound of walking sticks tapping the cobblestones outside our window. We rose quickly, packed, ate, and joined the little flow of pilgrims setting out for the mountain pass.

And then it was straight up through low-hung clouds.

For five kilometers.

To Hunto.

It is an abiding memory and it was repeated on many occasions: the brutal assault on lung and limb at the crack of dawn; out the door and up the mountain. Why? Because many villages we stopped at were nestled into valleys or on safe places on hillsides—hence the need to move up to get out and go on.

And on that morning, with only 780 kilometers left to walk, twenty-seven of them that day, my legs reminded me that I had spent most of the previous year living a sedentary life in a metropolis. I was fit because I did regular exercise during the year, but the steepness of the ascent was a shock to the system.

It was tough going.

After a short breather in Hunto, we kept going up. And after what felt like a lifetime, we broke through the clouds into a dazzling blue sky.

And there I am: sipping my tea, seated at the foot of the Virgin of Orisson, above the cloud line. She gazes down at me from 1,096 meters above sea level. She holds out her child, eyes cast downward, lovingly—a kindly being whose love extends to me and all who look to her. Ever so briefly, I, too, feel like her special child. I feel her love surpassing my understanding; I feel her wrapping her arms around me. I feel the warmth of the sun on my face and a deep contentedness inside me. My eyes fill with tears and it is hard to swallow. I notice that the blue of her inner robe matches the color of the sky—such a vast love.

We continued walking skyward. Mist gathered and swirled over the summer pastures as we followed the trail of pilgrims and day-trippers up the mountain, stopping briefly at a wooden cross. A simple barrier of four sticks tied together gave the monument a wide berth. There were lots of ribbons knotted around the makeshift enclosure. Stones and a few scallop shells had been placed at the foot of the cross. It was a lonely, misty spot.

Pilgrims had carried each one of these forlorn-looking objects up the mountain for a reason. I imagined they held the tears and prayers of the hopeful, the brave, the trusting, the faithful. Each had its own silent story. I bowed my head in acknowledgment and held my hand to my heart as I walked on by.

I don't remember crossing into Spain: the moment when one foot was in France and the other in Spain and then when both feet could go either way.

National boundaries are strange things. At what point does the language change and different rules apply? When you fly from one country to another, airports and security procedures tell you, loud and clear: *You are here—not there.* But when you walk across a border, there is nothing to tell you where you are. How do you know which bush is Spanish and which is French? Bushiness is not a national affair.

How do you know when you have crossed a boundary in a relationship?

How do you maintain healthy boundaries in your relationships with family? Friends? Colleagues?

Spain or not, I recognized a familiar feeling on unfamiliar territory. My body begged release from its burden; my mind alternately exhorted and cajoled it to go one more bend. And finally, joyous relief at being at the top of the Lepoeder Pass (1,410 meters).

There were cars and bicycles, hikers and pilgrims. And a decision to make. We could follow the road that wended gradually down to the Abbey of Roncesvalles, or we could take the quicker route straight down through the forest. We looked at the cars, smelled the fumes; looked at the number of people, heard their chatter, and headed for the forest. We read afterward that it was a dangerous decision. While the bandits of the Middle Ages no longer hid out among the trees, the steep descent had wreaked havoc on the joints and tendons of many an unwary pilgrim.

I knew only the exhilaration of literally bouncing down the mountain between oaks and beeches and firs over a carpet of leaves, soft and brown beneath my boots. We were Tigger and Pooh in the Hundred Acre Wood. Pooh sang one of his hums:

The birds sang.
We sang.
No, you didn't.
What then?

You huffed
and puffed
and bounced
all the way down
straight down
four kilometers.
Yes, that's right.
Straight down.

I loved it. There was no one but us. It was fun. It was crazy. But most of all, it was fast!

And then, there it was, the rooftop of the famous Abbey of Roncesvalles. A bit farther and we were at the door, looking for a bed for the night. The dormitories were full. Everyone spoke Spanish. No one spoke English. Or French. We got a room with a bathroom to ourselves.

The long journey across the top of Spain to Santiago had begun. Marcillac was two years behind us. I was no longer a rookie pilgrim, but my induction into El Camino Español started right there in Roncesvalles, just on the other side of the mountain—just over the border. We were definitely no longer in France.

That evening we attended a mass in the abbey church. I felt less like a pilgrim and more like a tourist watching a theatrical performance. The actors were robed in rich emerald. Their movements were beautifully executed, elegant against a backdrop of dripping gold. Their script-perfect voices were sonorous and melodious, lulling me with foreign sounds. I listened, fascinated, uncomprehendingly, for what may have been an hour. It was my introduction to the Spanish expression of Catholicism, more exuberant and colorful than what was behind me in France.

We moved on the following day to Biskaretta and Larrasoaña. Not far out of Roncesvalles, we were walking through woodland. I was well ahead of Richard—for once. I came to a very large, high iron gate that farmers use to keep livestock in and intruders out and stood in front of it, contemplating the various ways I could scale it, crawl under it, shove my gear through it, squeeze my body between its bars.

I was still scratching my head, ready to share my multiple thoughts and strategies with Richard, when he strode up, took one look at it, and without breaking stride opened it and walked straight on. I wish I could have seen my face as it dawned on me what had just happened. The only thing I hadn't thought about was actually looking for a handle. I hadn't seen it. It was on foreign territory! I had been so certain it would be a toughie to solve that I was convinced it would require an in-depth discussion.

Richard just threw a glance over his shoulder that said, *So what are you waiting for?* I started laughing so hard I couldn't stand up straight. Tears rolled down my face.

Pride in my super-practical Kiwi self was flung back in my face by an open gate. It was payback for the number of times I had scoffed at the intellectual but useless Frenchman. The Kiwi was flummoxed by a giant gate that wasn't even locked. The Frenchman just saw a handle and turned it. This was not the way it was supposed to happen!

My belief that Frenchmen, notably Parisians, were uniformly intellectuals and couldn't change a lightbulb if their life depended on it was formed early on in my life in France. Back in 1980, I was driving a Renault 5 down to Marseille from Paris when one of its tires got a puncture. Despite my liberal thinking around male and female stereotypes, I had always assumed that changing a tire on a car was an act performed by men, like my dad. Logically, then, I turned to the three young men accompanying me on this voyage south. All three, including my then husband, had degrees from France's top graduate schools. They represented the crème de la crème of France's intellectual elite. BUT they had studied history and philosophy and political science, not how to change a tire on a Renault 5.

I sat in the driver's seat watching them pore over the car manual looking for clues. They debated the pros and cons of various approaches to the problem without ever once checking what tools were actually available to perform the task. They had a marvelous time, all the while chuckling away at their ineptitude, as if it were something that went with the territory of the intellectually superior. I just wanted to get my dad out of bed in the middle of the night in New Zealand and say, "Will you please tell these froggies how to change a bloody tire!"

I eventually flagged down another motorist, who found the jack in the trunk and followed up with an excellent demonstration of how to change a tire. He'd probably left school at the earliest possible age! He received much acclaim from us all and waved us off to complete our journey to Marseille.

My intellectual approach to the farm gate told me how long I had been in France and how much its culture of reflection before action had rubbed off on me. I chortled all the way to Biskarreta, where we stopped for our first *bocadillo* lunch after Roncesvalles and before that night's stop in Larrasoaña.

> # Think of a time when the assumptions you had about someone proved to be wrong. How did you react?

Industrial Wastelands— Diamond Centers

Before continuing the story of our journey to Santiago, I want to tell you about something that in fact happened after we had completed our pilgrimage.

All the major towns on the Camino were surrounded by industrial wastelands that were a moral and physical struggle to walk through; they also all had old centers, architectural gems that made the effort worthwhile. But I want to focus on our experience of walking the industrial wasteland around Paris.

The Camino continued to teach us life lessons even after the pilgrimage had been completed. It is said that the real teachings of the Way begin once the pilgrim has turned her back to the setting sun in Fisterra—the *end of the earth and of the path—and turned her face toward the new day: the sun rising in the east. Once the pilgrim has turned toward the source of life—has bowed to the life force—the real pilgrimage can begin.*

In 2005, two years after we had reached the end of the path at the end of the earth in Fisterra, and one year after we had completed our journey at our official starting place of Conques, Richard and I had decided to walk the southern route, starting in Arles, crossing the Pyrenees from Somport, and meeting up with the main route—the route that we were on in 2002—at Puente la Reina, Queen's Bridge.

He had made careful plans, studying distances and finding overnight accommodations, when I put a spoke in Richard's wheel by accepting a job assignment in Buenos Aires. Rather than change his plans, he canceled everything, and I flew to Argentina with my client. As a compromise, I suggested we do what pilgrims of yore had done: close the door of their cottages and start walking westward. There is an adage that says the Camino starts at your back doorstep and finishes in Santiago. Most people today of course begin at official starting places like Le Puy-en-Velay or Vézelay or Arles.

For us, living in a suburb west of Paris, this new walk meant leaving the landing on the tenth floor and crossing the Seine and the Bois de Boulogne as the sun rose over one of Europe's biggest cities. The early morning rays picked up the leftovers from the previous night's work. We steered our boots around used condoms and dog poop in the Bois (the woods that make up the greenbelt around Paris) and headed into the empty August streets of old Paris.

At that time of year, on a beautiful day, walking through Paris was pure joy. I caught sight of myself in café windows and chuckled, delighted with the image of the authentic pilgrim setting out on another adventure. We were walking from home to Tours, some two hundred kilometers south of Paris.

We crossed under the Périphérique—the ring road that encircles the twenty arrondissements that make up the city of Paris—and headed into the southern suburbs via the green pathway, Chemin Vert. It is a nature walkway out of the city and into the suburbs that follows France's major southwest train line.

We slept the first night in the same hotel that I had used for years to run my coaching school trainings in Antony. My face was very familiar to the staff, but my attire did not match my usual image. "Different mission," I explained parsimoniously.

The following day we plunged into the heart of the industrial wastelands that grow up around any major town or city: more space, cheaper rent, close to the market, ease of transport, storage capacity, and devastatingly inhuman. The concrete concealed most traces of the track we were following. The map had not kept up with the rapid growth of the corrugated iron walls and the billboards. Ugliness does not lift up the soul. I had to call upon my moral reserves to keep my legs moving past the warehouses, gas stations, and mega retail stores.

Even when we found fields again, they came with barbed wire, detours, and unclear markings. The psychotherapeutic adage "the map is not the territory" was quite literally true. The territory was depressing. The map was useless. Even Richard the Reliable lost his way. We walked futile kilometers the wrong way. Car drivers were useless, and no one else was on foot or pony. It was a dismal, demoralizing day.

The day after that my water bottle burst.

The day after that we stayed with holier-than-thou Christians. Our answers to their religious probing sounded hollow and apparently fell short of the mark they had set for our souls. I secretly sighed and groaned but was too tired to care very much.

By the time we arrived in Chartres, on the fourth

day after closing the door to our apartment, I was fed up and regretting my great idea to walk from home to Tours. It was a poor substitute for the big plan to walk the southern route from Arles. My guilt over Argentina and Richard's anger over his plans being thwarted had both gone underground, and we were engaged in a compromise that neither of us fully believed in. The unspoken toxicity interfered with the flow of our endeavor. I wanted to quit but did not say so.

I knew Chartres well and had visited its magnificent Gothic cathedral many times. It was the destination of a pilgrimage in itself as well as being an important stop for pilgrims on the way to Santiago. There was too much history there for me: it was my first husband's hometown.

Then a strange thing happened. As with so many occurrences along the Way, there was no rational explanation for what happened to my right leg.

We had booked a hotel in the center of Chartres not far from the cathedral. The idea was to spend a rest day in the heart of the old town, recovering from the ordeal of exiting Paris before moving on to the next stage of our journey to Tours.

I went to get out of bed the following morning, but my right leg refused to function. I could put no weight on it without feeling intense pain. I could not stand. I could not walk. I lay there imaging all kinds of incurable afflictions. Richard displayed very little sympathy. I was locked up in a crime-and-punishment scenario. I had gone to Argentina. I had expiated my guilt. I had walked the wastelands. And now I couldn't walk. It felt biblical.

"I don't think I can go any farther," I whispered, adding, "I want to stop."

Richard agreed immediately, and it was as if a huge burden had been lifted from my shoulders. Somehow I'd had to be the one who gave up the quest. My release opened up the flow of words between us. We put the last four days behind us, and Richard returned to his preferred planner mode to come up with "Great Alternatives" to walking to Tours.

I swung both legs over the side of the bed and had walked to the bathroom before I realized a miracle had taken place.

These things happen on the Camino.

We took the train back to Paris and drove to the wine-tasting region of the Loire Valley.

Think about a close relationship
you are in or were in. Think about
what doesn't or didn't work in the
relationship.

Discuss with someone the scenarios
that had you playing victim, rescuer,
or persecutor—or all three.

Which is—was—your preferred role?

Why?

A String of Spanish Towns

From Larrasoaña, to Pamplona, to Puente la Reina, to Estella, to Los Arcos, to Viana, to Logroño, to Navarrete, to Nájera, to Santo Domingo de la Calzada, to Belorado, to Burgos.

Each town had its own history. Each hostel told a similar story. Each day was unique. We passed through Rioja vineyards lush with ripening grapes. We walked into chapels, churches, and cathedrals; each painted its own picture of the Bible, Spanish-style. Seen from my Protestant Methodist roots in New Zealand, the interiors looked like gaudy displays of blood and guts, agony and woe, and all in lurid colors. The founding stories of these buildings, when I could understand the language that described them, held my attention but didn't capture my heart. There was little attempt in most places to cater to a non-Spanish-speaking public, so I was left to my ragged memories of Spanish history and my fondness for the stories of Jesus.

Walking the Way in Spain that first year often felt a bit desultory: the path frequently ran alongside the main road; it took us through the inevitable industrial wasteland on the outskirts of every major town; it made no attempt to paint pretty pictures of itself for a tourist brochure.

I constantly had the impression that we were walking between the past and the present, tracing a line between the time of the Knights Hospitaller, an eleventh-century religious military order founded at the Hospital of Saint John of Jerusalem, and the motorways of the twenty-first century. We wore twenty-first-century Gore-Tex on our backs and carried slim, lightweight sleeping bags rolled up inside backpacks with padded backs and thick, shoulder-protecting straps. Our toiletries were squeezed into neatly designed plastic containers that could be refilled and safely carried aboard a plane if necessary.

We walked into villages built of stone walls going back to the Middle Ages. We walked along highways with trucks thundering along on our left side and insects going about their business in and among the wildflowers bordering fields of ripened crops on our right side. Cars whooshed and birds chirped and we walked between.

As pilgrims of the present, we followed the most accessible and safest routes traced by pilgrims of the past. Road builders in the twentieth century had followed the same routes for the same reasons: safety and accessibility. We, the pilgrims of the present, found ourselves with a choice as to where to direct our gaze: toward golden wheat fields or the slick lines of tar-sealed roads. Our ears had no choice. Sometimes the cacophony of trucks and cars was overwhelming. It had been different in France. Attention had been paid to aligning the path with major walking routes while still respecting the ancient passageways of the Camino. Or, rather, modern walkways had been traced with respect to the ancient path of pilgrims going to Santiago.

Whichever way it was, it meant we had been spoiled in France with nature's beauty, without the noise. We were able to benefit from the convenience of travel in the twenty-first century to get to the places where we could pretend, if we wanted to, to be pilgrims from the past. Spain offered no such pretense.

The modern Spanish pilgrim was mostly young, traveled in packs, and spoke loudly. At least they did in the hostels we stayed in. The Spanish contrasted dramatically in their attire with other European pilgrims.

They looked like they took the suffering of Christ literally. Their cross and crown of thorns manifested in their blisters from wearing cheap sneakers and thin socks; their back pains from carrying oversized rucksacks that contained their overweight sleeping bags.

I never found out if the suffering was part of the "fun" of walking the Camino with friends and family; whether it was an integral part of a pilgrimage, Spanish-style; or whether these pilgrims plain could not afford better equipment. I never found out because I couldn't ask them. I didn't speak Spanish. It was a rare experience to be in a country where so few people spoke English.

It had been like that in France when I first arrived in 1978. The French were so proud of their language that they forgave anyone making an attempt to speak it, but they were unforgiving of anyone who made the assumption that the world spoke English. Increasing the volume of one's speech in English on the grounds that any French person would therefore understand did NOT work. I learned quickly that a few words of French were worth a thousand words of English. But the French became international travelers, and conversing in English became part of the game, so they no longer looked down their long Gallic noses at anyone daring to address them in English on their native soil.

I got the impression that northern Spain was linguistically where France had been twenty years previously: proudly monolingual with no intention of changing. But I didn't know if it was an economic issue or a real choice. And being a proud race, would they have ever told me that they were too poor to travel anywhere else or in any other way?

I was just passing through and did not feel like making an effort, so I remained largely ignorant of the facts behind what I could observe of the boisterous young Spaniards filling the hostels with their chatter and their ill-adapted equipment. For a large number, the adventure of the Camino started only in Sarria, a town situated 100 kilometers from Santiago. The "rules" of pilgrimage stipulate that in order to qualify for your Compostela certificate, you must have proof of having covered at least 100 kilometers on foot. Sarria was the landmark departure point for many who tumbled out of taxis and hoisted their "crosses" onto their backs from there.

That first year in Spain, we sometimes gave ourselves a holiday by booking into a small hotel rather than condemning ourselves to another night of prudent promiscuity in an auberge espagnole. I found my levels of tolerance and forbearance severely challenged after several nights of sharing space with people I couldn't understand and whose customs and age didn't match my own. I felt guilty about this every now and then, but not enough to forgo the quiet luxury of a private bathroom and a good night's sleep.

Have you ever shared living space with people very different from you?

What were the biggest challenges?

While the contours of each day and night remain fuzzy, some of the memories of that period are razor-sharp.

Deep azure nylon curtains on bedroom windows of a small hotel in the center of the old town of Los Arcos. A light breeze made them sway delicately across an open window. The beauty of these simple curtains lulled me gently into a deep sleep, soothing the weariness in my bones.

Up early the following morning before dawn and leaning against the bar of the downstairs café. Filling the thermos and sipping a hot chocolate. My ears picked up the refrain of a Donovan number playing on the radio behind the bar. It was an old favorite about love being as hard to catch as the wind. I started humming along, feeling more and more wistful with each verse.

The lyrics took me back to a time when I was young, in love, insouciant, and still living in New Zealand, a world far away. I felt lonely now, before dawn, alone with my thoughts in a café with Richard and strangers. The words caught in my throat. Nostalgia threatened to suck my legs dry and leave me stuck on a barstool in Spain.

The song ended.

The sun rose.

Richard and I left the bar.

We started walking.

Memory followed: blue curtains catchin' the wind; words catchin' in my throat; you, so long ago, catchin' my heart.

Is there a particular song that takes you back to a world that was and makes you feel happy and sad at the same time?

Polarities

Spain was in economic recession in 2002. Buildings that people had had such high hopes for stood unfinished: roofs missing; walls still not plastered; cables dangling listlessly; rubble piled up; potholes gaping on unfinished footpaths. While the utterly demoralizing experience of walking through the industrial wastelands of Paris was not part of my brain's landscape at the time we were walking out of Pamplona or into Burgos or León, the encounter with the unattractive outskirts of each of these major Spanish towns was a disheartening affair.

Invariably there was a two- to three-hour hard slog in a straight line over concrete, around potholes, and between billboards. Without fail, the bag on my back mysteriously gained weight and my eyes tired from remaining glued to the ground to avoid tripping on something left at a building site.

We had made a vow back in April 2000 to walk all the way to Santiago, and by August 2002 we thought of ourselves as well-established pilgrims, so it never crossed our minds to take a bus into the center of town.

> **Are there promises that you have made to yourself that have caused you both joy and regret?**

Walking into a town through its unromantic out-skirts felt like a punishing prelude to the pleasure I anticipated experiencing on discovery of the diamonds at its heart. For me, having grown up in the New World, it was always exciting to travel back in time to the Old World. I loved to imagine how life used to be; to dream up stories; to take pictures from quaint hotels on narrow streets of thick stone walls; to be comfortable, well fed, and delighted with history.

We decided to stop in Burgos for a day of R&R. The old town met all the criteria!

We got a room with a view of the cathedral plaza. That night, with windows flung wide open, I lay in the luxury of a king-size bed covered with dazzling white sheets and watched the way the light of the moon—or maybe it was a street lamp—caught the carved stone of the cathedral's central portal: the door of forgiveness. I began dreaming before I fell asleep. It was blissful. The night slipped away.

The early morning light bounced off the stone walls again, and a cool breeze infiltrated our bedroom; we had left the windows open all night. I lay there, fully appreciating our extraordinary good fortune: to have a room with such a magnificent view of the diamond in the heart of Burgos.

The breakfast on offer was grandiose compared to our usual morning repast. We had it served in the room. I chose fresh peaches from Spain and yogurt from Greece, croissants à la française, and tea from my backpack.

The bathroom was all white and almost as big as the bedroom. I took a leisurely shower, sat on the edge of the bed, wrapped in a giant fluffy white towel with matching hair turban, watching a few people starting to gather outside the entrance to the cathedral. They were the type who got to places of interest early so as to enjoy the magic of the morning light and the silence before pack invasions of day-trippers began ripping the peace apart with their chatter and boisterous enthusiasm.

We joined the growing crowds a little later after breakfast, wandering idly along the narrow cobblestone streets of the old town around the cathedral until we came across an elegant-looking teahouse. Its well-polished wooden door had a stained glass inset. Pushing open the door, we stepped inside, full of anticipation.

The waiter had all the panache of a garçon in a Left Bank café, but I can still see the dumbfounded look on his face when I asked him what kind of tea he had.

"Tea," he replied. He pouted slightly, and there was doubt in his voice.

"Yes, but what kind?" I insisted with a smile.

"Tea is tea," he retorted, more sure of himself this time.

"Okay, I'll have tea then," I agreed, wondering why a waiter in a posh teahouse didn't know about the infinite varieties of black and green tea from all over Asia. But this was a coffee-drinking nation. Spain had conquered South America and inherited the coffee bean, not the tea leaf.

I had discovered long ago that the best way to disguise poor-quality black tea is to add milk or lemon to it, so in Spain I grew adept at requesting my morning tea *con leche*. I grew even more skilled after one waiter delivered a teapot full of hot milk with a tea bag on the side.

Seriously!

After that, when I ordered tea, I waited until it was set down on the table, feigned forgetfulness, raised my finger, eyebrow, and voice, and said with a note of regret, "Con leche?" The ploy ensured I would get tea in a pot and milk to add to it. It did not endear me to harassed waiters, but it did get me drinkable tea across northern Spain.

What I also got, in one or two places, thanks again to the Spanish colonial past, was divine hot chocolate.

I stood, in yet another coffee bar on yet another early morning, alongside a few other sunrise walkers. The café was in a plaza opposite a sixteenth-century church somewhere not far past Burgos. The bar was famous for its generous servings of hot chocolate. The church couldn't even begin to compete for my attention! I leaned over the bar, both hands clasped around a deep cup full of thick, rich, and barely liquid chocolate. The cup warmed my hands. I took small sips, and the chocolate slid smoothly and deliciously down my gullet. It fueled me and helped my legs move for the next ten kilometers.

In Burgos I'd foolishly ordered tea, not hot choco-late. We had left the "teahouse", climbed the steps, and entered the city's cathedral through its southern door. The inside was immense. I sat down, alone among the many visitors, and let the coolness of the stone walls soothe my soul. I felt the soaring Gothic architecture lift me upward. My muscles relaxed, my sense of space broadened, and all thoughts of what I had seen, done, eaten, drunk—and of what I wanted to see, do, eat, drink next—diminished in size. My whole being softened into a feeling of intense well-being. I lost all sense of chronological time. I had no idea how long this peaceful immersion lasted, but I knew Chronos had returned when thoughts of lunch and whatever might come next moved me to stand and continue my visit of the cathedral. I thought how wonderful it would be to prolong those spontaneous moments of unexpected bliss, and then I also thought I might never get lunch. My mind, true to its yo-yo nature, bounced up and down between the sublime and the commonplace.

**When, where, and with whom
have you experienced moments of
intense well-being?**

**How do these moments get
interrupted?**

Even though I was happy to get back on the road again, it was hard to say goodbye to the comfort of our hotel room and the beauty of the old town with the cathedral at its center. It was easy to adapt to comfort; tiresome to go back to roughing it. But in fact it was oscillating between the two that was most difficult for me. Once I got used to being on the road, I didn't miss the luxury of a thick mattress or fluffy white bath towels, but I never walked away from them without a twinge or a sigh of regret.

I gradually trained my mind not to hook onto thoughts of past or anticipated material comforts. I continued to enjoy a good cup of quality tea and to revel in the taste of a divine hot chocolate, but I didn't fret when they weren't available. I simply learned not to miss them. In fact, the real luxury turned out to be a balanced state of mind, regardless of circumstances.

How do you relate to loss of comfort?

What are you most attached to?

**What have you taught yourself to
let go of?**

From Burgos we walked to Castrojeriz.

We were preparing to cross the Meseta. It was important that we avoid finding ourselves in the middle of a desert-like landscape exposed to the torrid heat of a midday sun. We also had concerns about thunderstorms and the threat of lightning. Having heard tales of pilgrims struck by lightning while crossing, I assumed they had died from the experience; but I had never wanted to pursue that line of inquiry for fear of provoking too much anxiety within myself. I thought back to the charred remains of a horse I had seen, lying in an open field the summer before. It made me shudder instinctively as I imagined what a bolt of lightning might do to my own body. From the time I saw the dead horse, I consciously removed all jewelry from my body before walking across exposed terrain in thundery weather. Crossing the Meseta was a big deal in our minds. We were high up on a plateau and exposed to all the elements. We would be vulnerable if the weather turned bad.

We slammed the door of the hostel in Castrojeriz before sunrise on the morning of September 3, 2002, and stepped outside into pitch blackness. There wasn't a soul in sight. We realized in an instant that we didn't have a clue which way to turn: left or right? In all our worrying about storms and blistering heat, we hadn't given a thought to how dark it would be in our hostel's little narrow street before the first glimmer of dawn. We couldn't see the very familiar signpost showing the rays of a sunlike scallop shell on a blue background with an arrow pointing the way. We felt really stupid. Lightning flashed in the direction we were headed. The hostel door self-locked, so no way back. We felt worried as well as stupid. Richard fumbled around in his bag for his flashlight. We needed a flashlight to find the flashlight. Stupidity plus!

Another pilgrim left the hostel and headed authoritatively to his left. We feigned last-minute adjustments to our backpacks and quickly scuttled after him. We said nothing to each other about the mutual embarrassment of being mentally prepared for death by lightning but ill-prepared for being lost in darkness!

Worry took over from feelings of stupidity as first light showed a deeply troubled sky. Thunder rumbled and reached a crescendo as we got nearer to the top of the expected climb out of town. The lightning increased in frequency and brilliance. It was promising to be a display of biblical proportions, frightening and staggeringly beautiful. Great jagged streaks of purple-edged white light rent the remains of the night sky: slashing, crackling, irregular, oblique, and terrifyingly powerful.

I was truly frightened of what we were walking

toward. We tipped over the edge of the upward climb and onto the wide-open spaces of the plateau. I leaned into my fear and into a raging wind. Up here on the plateau, we were two tiny figures under the immensity of a low sky that boomed with electrical fury. There was nowhere to hide. I imagined death would come in an instant if it came as a bolt of lightning. We walked with deliberation: one foot followed the other without pause. My breath was even and focused; I was holding fear at bay. I prayed as I walked.

Do you pray?

When do you pray?

Why do you pray?

When the storm's energy was fully spent—rain never having come—the day settled into its early-morning, gracious self. The sun received our relieved faces and our gratitude with celestial indifference as it rose slowly toward midday, gaining infallibly in ferocity.

I felt genuinely relieved to have survived the storm without being fried alive or even getting wet, but we still had our destination to reach, and there was virtually no shade anywhere. I hunched my shoulders, pulled my hat down low over my eyes, and bent my head forward, chin tucked in. They were the only responses I had to a sun that, as it grew in strength, beat us mercilessly with its relentless rays. We trudged on toward our next stop in Frómista, not even stopping to sip tea.

From Frómista we moved on to Carrión de los Condes, followed by Calzadilla de la Cueza and then Sahagún.

Ah, Sahagún.

Postscriptum: I chose to call this episode "Polarities" because walking the Way in Spain in 2002 flung me from one extreme to another: from the sacred beauty of Burgos Cathedral and the divine comfort of a king-size bed to exposure to life-threatening elements on the Meseta; from the soul-destroying industrial wastelands around major towns to the picturesque diamonds in their old centers. The intensity of one extreme highlighted the experience of its opposite. Life was not bland on the road to Saint James! The choices of where to stay were all ours, but so much of what actually happened to us seemed beyond our control.

The storm up on the plateau had filled me with awe and made me feel small and vulnerable. I understood

why human beings had clustered and built shelters together; why people knelt in reverence to a power they
hoped would exert its will in their favor.

**Think about the polarities in
your own life.**

How do they operate?

Does one pole highlight the other?

**Do you reject one and seek to develop
the other?**

**Does anything change when you
embrace both poles?**

The Saga of Sahagún

Richard and I dealt with the ongoing ordeal of crossing the Meseta by sticking to a daily routine that had a certain rhythm to its structure:

> Up at dawn
> Roll the bag
> Pack the sack
> Bread and tea
> Out the door
> Walk walk walk
> Stop for tea
> Walk walk walk
> Arrive *albergue*
> Get the stamp
> Wash the socks
> Wash the body

Take a nap
Out for lunch
Spanish time
3:00 p.m.
Menú del día:
Pork and pudding
Back to hostel
Write the diary
Talk to pilgrims
Snack in kitchen
Lights out early

And so it went, day after day, in a rather pleasant way. The routine of our day fit with the nature of the terrain and the rhythm of the sun's movement across the sky.

We arrived in Sahagún in the early afternoon of September 6, 2002. We were only three days' walk from that year's destination, León. Richard had developed a large blister on the back of the heel of his left foot.

We made straight for the *albergue*, dropped our bags on that night's bunk, and followed our usual routine. At 3:00 p.m., when restaurants opened for the lunchtime service, we sat down and pointed to the few Spanish words we recognized on the menu. Our choices usually involved pork or chicken, and invariably we finished up with *arroz con leche*—rice pudding. It was no different that day.

After lunch, Richard decided to consult a doctor advertising himself as a specialist in treating the ills of weary pilgrims. He set off to see the doctor and I went back to the hostel. I expected him to pop into the doctor's surgery, get bandaged up, and be back in a jiffy.

The afternoon wore on, with no sign of Richard. I didn't have a clue where he was—other than "at the doctor's." Back in 2002, smartphones were not as vital as life itself, so we were not equipped for that kind of communication.

I just filled the time.

I sat around for a bit on my bunk opposite a lower bunk occupied by an oldish, wiry chap with thin, muscular arms and well-worn boots. His hair was thinning on top and he had a ruddy complexion, with skin that was beginning to resemble a walnut shell. We got into conversation. I noticed how his eyes gleamed as he recounted the number of times he had walked the Camino.

There was no else around in the large room that afternoon, and I couldn't help but remember a tale I had been told about the demons who frequented the trail, posing as pilgrims. They were always old but fit men. They always walked over forty kilometers a day. They always had gleaming, beady eyes, and they never left the path. They roamed up and down the Way, preying on the innocent.

I didn't feel all that innocent at fifty, but I had never thought to ask what kind of preying they did or what kind of shape their victims were in once they had been preyed upon.

I remained jocular but did not feel at ease. I tried as casually as I could to inquire into the number of kilometers he had done that day, the number of times he had walked the Camino, whom he had been walking with, and whether they were staying at the same hostel as we were.

Sure enough, he HAD done over forty kilometers that day, AND he HAD walked the Way many times, AND he WAS traveling alone. I wished I'd had sunglasses on so I could really stare at his gleaming eyes, imagining I could work out if they held unholy intentions or not. I wanted to study him more carefully, given he would be sleeping so close to me that night.

I wished there was someone else around.

I wished Richard would hurry up and get back.

The afternoon light grew dimmer inside the room, and I had exhausted all my conversational ploys. I didn't want to draw attention to myself in any unnecessary way, and I definitely wanted to get out of there before it got too dark to see clearly from one bunk to the next. I stood up, looked at my watch, and feigned shock. "Heavens!" I exclaimed. "My husband will be waiting for me downstairs. Do excuse me."

I left all my gear unattended on the bed and headed down, knowing full well Richard was not back yet. I never saw the man again. I don't know where he slept the night, but it was not in the bunk opposite mine. Had I had a lucky escape, or was my imagination working overtime because I was starting to get anxious about Richard's nonappearance?

I headed to the kitchen, where there were more people. Richard was not among them.

I prepared the evening snack for us both in his absence. It was dark by then. I tuned in to the voices around the communal table. One voice in particular irritated me intensely. It was that of a young woman with very familiar intonation: strident, dominating, authoritative. Everything I knew I could be and didn't like: the bossy headmistress who knows it all. Worse, she expounded on Asia, where I had traveled the hippie trails for months, back in the seventies. "Teach your grandmother to suck eggs," I muttered ungraciously under my breath.

A demon in the bunk room, a harpy in the kitchen, and still no Richard. I felt rattled. I paced around outside but could not find any sort of peace within myself. I was irritated. I was worried. I had nowhere to go. Nothing to do except wait.

I went down to the hostel lobby, where there were a couple of computers available. I might not have had a smartphone back in 2002, but I did have an email account, and I thought I would try to occupy my mind by logging in and sending a few messages. I could not get into my account. I could feel the rage building in me, the desire to smash the stupid machine to smithereens: to kill it, murder it, remove it forever from the face of the earth. I was about to go off the Richter scale completely when I looked across to the other computer and saw someone working happily away on it.

That one worked.

Then I realized it was one of two Belgian nurses who were traveling the Way together. We had shared many a bunkhouse with them, and I knew by now to make sure I had a bed as far away from them as possible.

They snored.

Atrociously.

I never woke myself up snoring, so it is irrelevant to this story whether I ever kept anyone else awake with my nocturnal purring.

I said nothing. I fumed.

Then suddenly, there was Richard in the entranceway. He was grinning. I was relieved and beside myself with frustration. The one word I was capable of summoning came out more as a snort. "So?"

He said, "The doctor has told me to rest for a day."

He might just as well have said, "We will be shot at dawn."

I glared at him in furious disbelief. Another day here in Sahagún with demons and harpies, dead computers and snoring Belgian women! Every muscle in my body was pulled taut with seething rage. Before I could say anything else, I heard the sugary tone of a woman's voice over my shoulder. I whirled around and caught the simpering smile of the Belgian directed at Richard. She gazed into his eyes and said softly, "I am a nurse. Can I help you?"

Well, that did it.

That tipped me over the edge.

"No, you bloody well can't," I fired at her through clenched teeth.

Richard looked at me in disbelief, quickly divined the atmospheric pressure around us, grinned sheepishly at her, and proceeded to follow me meekly up the stairs to the bunk room without another word being said—by anyone!

I didn't explain why his having a blister the size of an apple on his heel, or why being told by a doctor that it would be wise to rest for a day, or why the offer of help from a nurse would provoke such a violent outburst from me. I only knew that I was going to be jailed for another day against my will, and that it was his fault. Every cell in my body smoldered with pent-up fury.

When I woke the following morning, I was still under the spell of thwarted will and its power to ignore all reason. I still had enough anger in me to keep any feelings of guilt at bay. I did, however, avoid crossing paths with the nurse at the breakfast table. The demon, the harpy, and the Belgian women moved on and we were left in an eerie, silent hostel.

We spent the morning at the local market. Richard wore open-back sandals. I felt vengeful. I felt reckless. I was carrying a cell phone that had a calling plan that only included Europe. I made three long calls to New Zealand. I called my mother. I called my sister. I called my brother. It cost a fortune and I didn't care.

The madness that had so disturbed my equilibrium eventually started to dissipate. The melodies of home had pulled me back to my familiar self. As I meandered through the market, not really seeing what I was idly looking at, I did begin to see how I had been con-sumed by an old pattern of mine: raging anger that ripped through anything that got in its way, including all feelings of despair and helplessness when the world slipped totally outside my control.

Richard's blister, Richard's absence, the computer not working, the boasting, stupid woman in the kitchen, the strange man in my bunk room, nightfall, and finally a nurse who could help where I could not. I sighed and thought how easy it would be to put my craziness down to a demon on a bunk bed.

By afternoon Richard thought he would be okay to move on. I didn't know if he was saying that to please or appease. I was no longer angry, but I couldn't gauge to what extent he had decided to assume his pain in order to placate my frustration.

We moved on, sweating under the weight of our backpacks in the heat of an unforgiving sun.

Now here is a very strange thing: After about three kilometers we got to a small bridge and stopped to catch our breath and mop our brows. I suddenly realized I did not have my precious leather hat that I had started out with two and a half years ago. How it was possible for me to walk in the heat without realizing I did not have my hat I will never know. The thought of walking back to Sahagún to get it was excruciating. The thought of going on without it was like losing a best friend. I started to cry. All the emotion of the past twenty-four hours accumulated in the loss of my hat. Richard said he would go back and get it for me. That really made me cry. For a while I just sat there, hatless.

And then, as if from nowhere, a fellow pilgrim came toward us, held out my hat, and said, "You left this behind at the hostel."

I was speechless. I was also emotionally exhausted and could not work out how he had known it was mine or where he would find me. It didn't make sense that he was also walking in the full heat of day when everyone else had left the hostel early in the morning. I didn't recognize him, and I couldn't explain why he was there, but he had my hat and I was deeply grateful.

I didn't understand.
I did feel ashamed of the previous day's behavior. I heaved a huge sigh, placed my hat on my head, lifted my pack onto my shoulders, and stood ready to move on.

The spirit does indeed move in mysterious ways, and maybe demons come in many guises, not all of them harmful.

Think of a time when you didn't get what you wanted. What did you do?

Now think of a time when you did get what you wanted. What didn't you do?

Transitions: From Backpack to Beach— Pilgrim to Holidaymaker

There were just three days more to walk to León after Sahagún. The walk to Calzadilla de los Hermanillos, our next stop after Sahagún, was relatively short, but we had time enough to mull over the events of Sahagún and the craziness that had turned me, momentarily, into an uncompassionate monster. A further day's walk to Mansilla de las Mulas gave me time to also process the disconnect between abominable behavior toward a loved one and unexpected kindness and consideration from a stranger.

I had been brought up on the golden rule: "Do unto others as you would have them do unto you." It no longer hung together as a neat and tidy equation. Strictly speaking, according to this rule, at least as seen with a child's logic, I could expect retaliative behavior from Richard and I should return kindness to an unknown person.

By the time we reached León, on the third day after Sahagún, the parable of the Good Samaritan, and the mercy he had shown someone in need despite this someone's being his traditional enemy, made real sense to me.

The stranger's kindness and my fury toward Richard and his blister were two unconnected events, but their juxtaposition in time and space, and the time I had to think about them after Sahagún, offered me one of the great teachings of the Camino: simple acts of kindness toward others, whoever they are, heal things other than blisters.

Have you ever met a Good Samaritan? When?

Have you ever been a Good Samaritan to someone else? When?

On September 10, 2002, we left León and took a train to Hendaye, in France. After a month of walking, we transitioned in the space of a day from pilgrim to holidaymaker; from following a trail on foot to lying on hot sand and swimming in the sea; from carrying our house on our backs to living in a rented apartment.

It wasn't difficult to move into holiday mode. I swam a kilometer before breakfast instead of walking twenty-five of them in a day. I enjoyed loafing on the beach with a good thriller to keep me company.

It wasn't the R&R that marked the transition from the Way to the beach; it was the fact that we became, once again, strangers among strangers. The spontaneous and natural camaraderie that we experienced among pilgrims was something that made us feel like we belonged to a community of brothers and sisters from many families and nations. At the beach on holiday, Richard and I became a happy, isolated little unit of two again.

And to vacation was to enter into a vacant spot, without the clear framework either of the daily life of a pilgrim or of a professional woman running her own business in Paris. I was not sleeping, eating, walking at a religiously regular pace; nor was I rushing to get through a Paris traffic jam to catch a plane or a train.

I was somewhere in between.

And from where, in time, this story is being told, a vacant space is exactly what COVID-19 has created. An invisible creature showed up in all our lives and decided it wanted to live in our lungs. It suffocated some of us and left the rest of reeling from a totally unplanned-for transition.

Cities, emptied of cars and people, naturally replenished their air supply. Birds and other fauna appeared on the vacated streets. We noticed them because there was time available to do so. Many people died for want of air, but those who survived without falling ill learned to love fresh air and the small things in life.

And this, to come back to my story in 2002, reflects the life of the pilgrim: having time to fall in love with the small things—to notice the way the early morning light catches the spiderweb woven in glistening threads between fence wires; to gaze into the heart of a buttercup brazenly, brilliantly yellow among sheaves of emerald grass; to watch the way the wind ruffles the leaves of trees; to catch the quiet music of the land at eventide.

In July 2000, I had fallen in love with Hendaye's beautifully carved three kilometers of sand and surf on first sight. It required no effort to embrace its lovely curves again in September 2002. My feet had a newfound sensitivity to the coolness of wet sand; the roughness of tiny broken seashells; the slimy slipperi-ness of seaweed and the salty kissing movements of sea-foam carried forward with each incoming wavelet.

We would return to the Way the following year to finish what we had started.

**What has helped you transition
in and out of a world, in and out
of lockdown?**

PART 5 SPAIN
2003 SUMMER

Let He Who Is Without Sin Cast the First Stone

We took a train back to Spain, arriving in León on August 8, 2003. We stayed one night and collected our first stamp on the night of August 9 from Villar de Mazarife. I felt fit and healthy and ready to begin the last long leg of the journey. I also felt settled within myself, as if nothing much could rock the boat. I was an old hand at the pilgrim business by then, and there was plenty of time in front of us. Richard had again done his research into daily distances and possible hostels to aim for every afternoon. We would only stay in hostels, which meant we would aim to arrive at the door of the hostel in question before it opened, drop our backpacks in the queue, and wait patiently for the doors to open so we could sign in and choose a bunk for the night.

Sleeping every night in a Spanish hostel would test my tolerance of human behavior. I would sleep through severe neon lighting, raucous laughter, flushing toilets, and volcanic snoring. I would feel compassion for fellow travelers: for their aches and pains and complaints.

And so it began.

We passed from León to Castile and into Galicia; into bagpipes and flutes and Celtic roots.

Whenever I hear bagpipes or see a Scottish marching band, tears well up and a lump in my throat prevents me from speaking. The plaintive wailing sounds of the pipes call me back to some faraway place and time that I feel a yearning for. My grandfather was from Glasgow. He left a poor family in Scotland as a young boy, went to New Zealand, married my grandmother, had two little girls, and died of lung cancer when my mother was eighteen months old, at the time of the Great Depression. He was just twenty-eight years old. Perhaps it is my mother's sadness I feel when the piper squeezes his tartan bag and begins his long, slow, continuous, undulating lament.

I heard the baggies in the narrow stone streets of O Cebreiro at the gateway to Galicia, 1,300 meters above sea level and 156 kilometers from Santiago. I was a long way from home. I eased my backpack off my shoulders and leaned against a stone wall. My eyes brimmed with tears. No one noticed me. It was the sort of thing that happened to weary pilgrims, and no one paid any particular attention. Richard was wandering the narrow streets, exploring—anyway, he knew my soft spot for the baggies, so would not have been in the least bit concerned had he seen me, head down, quietly sobbing.

Before reaching the gateway to Galicia and the final 156 kilometers, we first had to pass through Hospital de Órbigo, Astorga, Rabanal, El Acebo, Ponferrada, Villafranca del Bierzo, and a hostel in a town whose stamp is smudged except for the date, which states that I was there on August 16, 2003.

In Astorga I dangled my feet in a paddling pool for pilgrims at the hostel where we stayed. I sat on a long stone ledge alongside that day's traveling companions. Although only my aching feet and tight calves were immersed in the cool, gurgling, bubbling waters of the canal-like pool that ran along the back stone wall of the hostel's courtyard, I felt the fatigue of the day slowly ebb away from my shoulders and back and even my jawline. It was unmitigated bliss. My mind drifted idly along with the current. I thought about the symbolism of washing someone else's feet.

My beautician did it, but I paid her to do it, and she tarted up my toenails while she was at it.

I thought about the biblical symbolism of Christ washing his disciples' feet at the Last Supper. He, the great teacher, stooping and kneeling in front of his beloved disciples, washing their feet, before events took hold of them all. I imagined Him saying, "I am your servant and your teacher. The esteemed as well as the lowly receive their power from my Father in Heaven. Let this act of humility be your teacher."

While I was impressing myself with these thoughts, the skin of my feet turned prune-like and my calf muscles slowly rigidified. With difficulty, I extracted myself from the pool and hobbled over to where my open-toe sandals were waiting for me.

Ever since my Sunday school years, I have loved the stories of Jesus and his band of brothers, who for a short period, stirred up the status quo in Palestine. He seemed to have had a lot of love and respect for women. I would like to have grown up with him as my brother, but I would have skipped the ending.

While I knew that our destination, as for all on this pilgrimage, was the tomb of Saint James in Santiago, I had never given much thought to the questions that suddenly occurred to me now: Why James? Why Spain? Why Galicia, in particular? I knew that James was one of Christ's chosen twelve, but I hadn't known that he had preached the Word in Spain, returned to Palestine, and had his head chopped off by Herod. His body was sent on a boat back to Spain, where it washed ashore in Galicia.

The story goes that his remains were buried in a field and forgotten about until a shepherd a few centuries later rediscovered them. The shepherd was "guided" to the spot by the brightness of a light on an otherwise dark night over that particular patch of ground. A great cathedral was erected on the site, becoming the epicenter of one of the world's major pilgrimages. The discovery, incidentally, contributed to a need for the Catholic kings and queens of Castile to reinforce the northern boundaries of their kingdom and those of Christendom against further incursions into their territory by Arab invaders. The Camino—the Way—was a convenient shield that the Order of Santiago, another religious military order, could defend, quite legitimately. The knights of the order became engaged in feeding, housing, and protecting pilgrims on their way to pay homage to Saint James.

The hostel in Astorga was the only place we stayed along the Way that offered the absolute luxury of soaking one's feet at the end of the day's walk for an unlimited amount of time. I would expect nothing less in heaven.

The climbing in the León mountains was tough,

arduous, relentless. My knees suffered from the effort of supporting eighty to ninety kilos between them day after day, my weight plus what I was carrying.

I particularly remember the mountain village of Foncebadón because of the trepidation with which I approached it. I had read a book by Shirley MacLaine in which she described her adventures on the Camino. In Foncebadón she had met ferocious giant dogs that had made her passage across the village a very hairy affair. Even on the outskirts of the village I was afraid of what we might have to deal with. I mustered all my strength in anticipation of a confrontation with savage dogs. My knuckles went white from gripping my stick so hard. My eyes swiveled in all directions. Richard and I stopped speaking. My jaw tightened, and the adrenaline started pumping from the moment the first huts, hovels, and houses appeared. My ears were on high alert. Had I been wearing sandals and not heavy walking boots, I would have held my breath and tiptoed all the way across to the other side of this small village so as not to awaken the man-eating mastiffs.

Was it to be flight or fight?

Richard went first.

I followed.

The village was silent.

Nothing.

I was exhausted by the time we made it to the other side of the village—without any sign of any kind of dog. My head and neck ached from the tension. I was relieved to have "survived" an ordeal that never happened.

I have always wondered whether MacLaine made up the story about the dogs, or whether the few inhabitants of Foncebadón, in response to an increase in pilgrim traffic, had "silenced" their wild dogs. I never found out, but I also never forgot the place.

> **Are you afraid of dogs? If yes, where might this fear come from?**
>
> **Are there any animals that frighten you?**

From Foncebadón there was a steady climb to the highest point on the Camino: Mount Irago, with its Cruz de Ferro (iron cross) atop a giant tree trunk. At the foot of the pole that held the cross was an enormous mountain of rocks and stones. Many had messages written on them or jammed underneath. There were all sorts of other little mementos tucked in among the cumulus that had been left there over time by thousands of pilgrims on their way to Santiago.

The sky hung low that day, and there was some mist and dampness in the atmosphere. We rested a while at a forlorn altitude of 1,504 meters above sea level and got a sense of how much human glumness had accumulated in this spot. I had read that a pilgrim could atone for a sinful act by carrying a stone representing his sin in his backpack and placing it at the foot of this cross. The heavier the stone, the greater the sin and the more significant the act of atonement. I had also read that it was an ancient tradition among the Roman occupiers and local herdsmen to leave a stone as a way of calling on the gods to protect them as they made their way down the treacherous mountain track on the other side. Both versions moved me to think about my relationship to sin, to God, and to the terrain we were crossing.

Back when I was young enough to think that my father had godlike powers, I was taught right from wrong through a simple equation: crime = punishment. I put a tennis ball through the backyard window, smashing it to pieces, and my father gave me a hiding when he got home from work that night. My playing tennis against the back wall of the house wasn't a crime, but my dad probably resented having to find the money to replace the windowpane. There wasn't any spare cash to go around when I was a kid. That beating was a bit unfair, because it was more about his frustration than my behavior.

However, I really deserved the hiding I got when our neighbors got back from their holiday and found their backyard garden decimated.

The boy next door and I had gone on a gleeful wrecking spree in their absence and got a bit carried away. I can still remember, though, the unmitigated thrill of ripping out all their summer vegetables, smearing their backdoor step with boot polish, and removing all the nails from their son's go-cart so the whole thing fell apart.

I then lived in abject fear, waiting for the neighbors to come back.

It took them three days.

I was in purgatory, waiting for someone to tell my father what I had done. They did.

I got yanked out of bed late on the third night and got the hiding of my life.

It put an end to my budding bent toward delinquency. The agony of not knowing if I would get caught, and what my dad would do to me if I was, was far worse than the pain of the punishment when I did get caught. And the two together far outweighed the thrill of committing the crime. I didn't feel any guilt about what I had done. I had indeed loved every moment of it while I was doing it.

I wondered, as I sat at the Cruz de Ferro on August 16, 2003, if you needed to feel guilty to feel as if you had sinned. If that was the case, I was looking at an awful lot of human guilt and misery, given the sheer number of rocks piled up at the foot of this iron cross.

There was one other memory that came back to me as I mulled over what this high point on the road meant to me.

While I remained capable of giggling at the thought of wrecking the neighbors' property, stealing from a girl at primary school still filled me with shame sixty years later.

We were both stamp collectors and swapped stamps during recess. We both had beautifully kept albums and competed with each other to get the best collection. I recognized the value of one of her stamps from what one of my older cousins had told me. It was a dull brown, with the king of England's head on it, and it had several little regular pinpricks in it. It was this that was said to give it value. I told my friend a cock-and-bull story about the value of one my worthless but brightly colored stamps and said I was willing to give it to her in exchange for the stamp with the holes in it. She found it a bit strange, but she trusted me. We were friends, after all. I remember the triumph I felt when she agreed and the stamp came into my hands.

Only I knew what I had done. No one would tell, and I would not be punished. But I was punished.

I regret, all these years later, cheating a friend. I was young, yet old enough to know what I was doing. It was only a stamp, but I could easily have righted the wrong by just giving it back to her and telling her she should keep it because it was valuable. I didn't. I have no idea what happened to that stamp or the album it belonged to, but the memory still pricks my conscience.

Yes, I thought, *this slimy wee deed is probably worth a stone on the mount's heap.*

I noticed a few people clambering up this make-shift pile of human burden and wondered why they felt the need to do that. It seemed to me they were treading over the pain and hopes of all those who had left a little piece of themselves on that heap. I didn't feel tempted to wade through so many memories, in spite of the splendid view that was promised from the top. Maybe if the weather had been better, I might have been tempted. I could see how easily my wanting something badly enough could make me forgo the high moral ground I liked to walk on.

Instead I left a message for a far more recent friend than the one from my primary school days, scribbled on a piece of paper I tore out of my diary. I displayed it on a rock and held it down with four smaller stones. If it didn't rain and the wind didn't blow too hard AND the local gods were smiling favorably, she would find it. She was walking with her father, and by my reckoning, they were just two days behind us. Her father had cancer. Maybe they were carrying stones that would slow them down.

And then it was time to move on down the mountain to a hostel in a town whose name I do not remember.

What does "to sin" mean to you?

What "crimes" have you committed in your life that would merit a stone at the foot of the Cruz de Ferro, and what size might that stone be?

Getting There

From the town whose name I can't remember, we passed though O Cebreiro, with its haunting melodies, narrow streets, and stone houses, to Triacastela, where we stayed in another albergue the night of August 17. The following day we walked on to the monastery of Samos, where we stayed the night of August 18.

Once inside its walls we were pulled, whether we liked it or not, into the deep Catholic roots of the pilgrimage. We accepted the traditional free night's accommodation and meal afforded any pilgrim on his way to the tomb. I felt, as a woman in a sanctuary for men, that I did pay a small price: that of a round peg in a square hole. I didn't belong, and that was not a comfortable feeling.

The silence during dinner, not unusual in a house of worship, felt forced rather than gracefully accepted.

A woman with a scowling face served the dinner that evening. She was one of the ancient residents dressed in black who crept the corridors of the monastery, oozing obsequiousness. Her presence successfully contributed to my sense of not really feeling welcome. I felt insignificant to an exaggerated degree.

Perhaps I was picking up on the weight of generations of men living without women within the monastery's walls. Maybe not only I had feelings of insignificance. Perhaps these bent old women were symptomatic of what needed to change after over a thousand years of domination. Just possibly, it was seething resentment, under layers of subservience, that I couldn't help but feel. Not only was I not really welcome in a male sanctuary, but I was also most likely resented as a free woman by my seniors, who had not had the same choices I had had. I could not blame them for not wanting to serve me with graciousness at the table, but I couldn't wait to get out of there the following morning. The cost of a night's stay was too high despite the monastery's illustrious reputation for hospitality.

Have you ever found yourself in a situation where you did not feel welcome?

What do you know of feelings of rage or hatred that accompany rejection or exclusion?

Samos was the only place along the Way where I felt the unbalanced, dominating male energy of the Catholic Church. I wondered if a monastery was the only place men could feel safe from domineering mothers. I wondered if the only safe way for a monk to worship his mother was to put her on a pedestal and call her Mary, mother of God. The religious and cultural tradition I was born into, Protestantism, had dispensed with the female form altogether. I wondered if this could explain the need for men to find refuge from women in their men-only clubs and pubs. I have a son. I wondered if he needed to find a "safe" place away from his mother. Whom would he choose as his partner in life, a man or a woman?

He would choose a woman, as it turned out, convert to Judaism, and have two daughters. He would say he agreed to circumcision in order to belong fully to a community with deep historical roots. He would join the liberal American Jewish community in Paris. So he would convert to a religion that traditionally only recognized those born to Jewish mothers as being Jewish. Liberalism would be my son's sanctuary, and men and women would all be welcome.

Where do you find sanctuary when you need it?

From Samos we walked on to Sarria, the famous watershed 100-kilometer landmark. By then the Way had transformed into a highway of hopeful pilgrims. The end was in sight. Hopes were high, buoyancy in everyone's step.

It was true that there were taxis and buses that spewed their loads of wannabe pilgrims out onto the trail. These people would perform the perfunctory 100 kilometers required to obtain a Compostela in Santiago. I had no particular judgment to make on their choice of starting point, but I did have a vague concern about where everyone was going to find a bed for the next few nights.

The closer we got to Santiago, the more stamps we collected along the way, as if each place were anxious that we remember the role it played in a journey drawing to a close. I have two stamps from Portomarín; one only from de Palas de Rei; and three on the same day, August 22, from O Abrigadoiro, Furelos, and Melide. Their names were exotic; my experiences of these places, less so.

Although . . .

Melide was three days out of Santiago.

I see, in my mind's eye, a monolithic, antiseptic hostel with neon lighting. The place is overrun with eager, mostly Spanish-speaking pilgrims. In the center of town on a hot night, a giant platter of octopus is eaten by pilgrims seated on two long benches.

Despite Melide's not even being on the coast, it was famous for its octopus. People came from everywhere to tuck into chewy tendrils fresh out of boiling pots of water.

Richard could not look at the live octopuses slithering around in giant buckets without feeling slightly nauseated. Personally, I preferred not to think too much about slimy suckers or squirming tentacles once they were served. They came to the table steaming hot, chopped, salted, and sprinkled with a little olive oil and freshly squeezed lemon juice, and were set in front of me on a huge round wooden platter. The serving was generous, without trimmings. My teeth sunk easily into each morsel, and chewing was an effortless exercise in unadulterated pleasure.

It was Richard's turn, in Arzúa, the town after Melide, to experience the culinary delights of the area. Guidebooks told us there were more cows here per capita than anywhere else in Galicia, and we dutifully dined on the area's famous Arzúa-Ulloa cheese presented in a variety of ways. My memory doesn't stretch to include the finer details of each dish we tried.

Our arrival in Santiago had deep meaning for us, and I think that these excursions into local specialties helped us prolong the experience of the Way after four years of personal growth and adventure. It was as if neither of us really wanted it to be over—but we couldn't identify or name what we were feeling, so we tucked into those last few days with touristic gusto.

It rained the night of August 24. We were up before dawn on the morning of the twenty-fifth. It was the day we would pass through the ancient walls of the old town of Santiago and head for the tomb of the saint—our destination, and the end of our pilgrimage.

I'd had a strange dream, the kind where the

boundaries between waking and sleeping states are not clearly delineated. I awoke slightly confused as to what was real and what was not. In the dream, I was crossing an arid, russet-red landscape. Far in the distance I could see a sheer gray cliff face, wet with rain, rising high into a vivid blue sky. At the top was a city of tall buildings made of rose-colored Jerusalem stone. The outlines of the cliff and the buildings were cut against the sky. I don't remember the details of the dream, but I do remember the deep sense of peace that pervaded it. I remember the strange sensation and thoughts I had upon waking—the certainty that I had been blessed and that all would be well.

The bunk bed, the walls of the hostel, and my backpack were exactly as they had been the night before, but my dream had been so "real" that my body felt strangely out of place. We laced up our boots, skipped breakfast, and stumbled out into the predawn darkness.

We got lost!

Our torchlights didn't show up any of the famous Way markers. We wandered aimlessly for about twenty minutes until the first rays of light. It was odd, given the huge number of pilgrims on the road by then, that we had not seen anyone we could have followed. I was still in the embrace of my dream, so I was unconcerned about not having a clue where I was.

Richard remembers the smell of eucalyptus. I remember the smell of pine. Both smells were made pungent by the previous night's downpour. But I am convinced that we walked through a forest of bamboo. The confused memories are symptomatic of the general confusion surrounding the beginning of that momentous day. Four years and three seasons of walking were drawing to a close.

The outskirts of Santiago were no more attractive than any other urban periphery we had trudged through in the past, but, knowing that this was the last leg, not even the hideous structure atop the Hill of Joy, or Monte do Gozo, could daunt our spirits. We stopped to gape at the huge block of inscribed stone, a monolith that holds two mighty swirls of bronze that in turn support a huge cross with a giant scallop shell at its center. On either side is a statue of a pilgrim. From the Hill of Joy, which comes into view directly before one sees traces of the city's crumbled medieval walls, pilgrims are meant to catch their first glimpse of the three spires of the apostle's cathedral. It is from this vantage point that their joy is said to overflow and their knees to give way with gratitude. This did not happen to me, but I was quite pleased to sit down and take a break.

The spires were lost in urban sprawl. And a monument that had been built to celebrate Pope John Paul II's visit in 1989 was a rusting monster of Stalinist dimensions by the time we got to gape at its ugliness in 2003. On World Youth Day 1989, thousands upon thousands of young people had gathered on the hillside to listen to the pope's final address. Rows and rows of bungalows, built to accommodate them, covered much of the hillside and proved an excellent response to pilgrim overflow in Jacobean jubilee years—when Saint James Day, July 25, falls on a Sunday.

But the young people all went home in 1989 and left the sculpture to rot in isolation like one of Shakespeare's tragic kings.

We walked on.

And then we were there, in the square, in a throng.

Before the doors of Saint James of Compostela.

Santiago— August 25, 2003

We entered the Santiago de Compostela Cathedral through the main doors along with many others, pilgrims and tourists alike. And then Richard and I entered our private spaces and, without exchanging any words, drifted apart to commune in whatever way we each felt moved.

I was stopped in my tracks by the opulence of the cruciform interior. My head tipped backward and my mouth dropped open as my eyes sought to take in the sheer size and splendor of the barrel-vaulted nave and broad transept; the organ, choir, and portals. There was too much to absorb immediately. I was overwhelmed visually but slightly disappointed that I was not overcome by feelings of joy or gratitude at having finally reached our destination: the end of the pilgrimage.

I was standing there thinking all this when I caught sight of Richard sitting alone in a pew in his muddy boots and grubby T-shirt. I was close enough to see his lips trembling uncontrollably. He was sobbing his heart out. This was his arrival. It was his private event that I would witness but not be a part of. We had traveled together, but we arrived alone. I wondered if that would be a fitting epitaph on our respective tombstones: "We traveled together, but we arrived alone."

The only other time I know of that Richard cried, his heart fit to break, was when his father died. The only witnesses were his father's third wife, Richard's first wife, and his two children. I was not present. He told me later that he had been overcome by a deep sense of loss and loneliness and regret for something that was gone forever.

In Santiago he felt, he said later, a not dissimilar sense of finality spilling out of his heart, running down his cheeks as he sat in the pew. He was so close to the tomb of Saint James, which we had traveled so far, for so long, to reach.

I sat down in a pew nearby, looking without seeing anything very much. My thoughts drifted until they settled on a time many years earlier when I was again in the heart of the holiest of the holy: the Church of the

Holy Sepulchre in Jerusalem.

It was Good Friday. I was alone—or so I thought. A bearded man in a black cassock appeared at my side. I felt instant gratitude toward this holy man who chose to be beside me as I witnessed the place where Christ's body was said to have been placed. I could not believe my good fortune at being able to commune in silence in the presence of one whose life must have been devoted to the sacraments. I smiled at him in silent acknowledgment of his presence at this most privileged moment of my life.

He came closer, until we were standing shoulder to shoulder and the tomb of Christ was staring at us both.

Suddenly his hand reached out from under his cassock.

It grabbed my left breast.

I caught the undisguised leer on his face in the dim light, the odor of sweaty arousal suddenly palpable.

In a second, I realized I was in danger—and paralyzed. I was too stunned to respond.

Lack of response was taken for acquiescence.

I saw his right hand begin to move.

I suddenly snapped into action and fled the holiest shrine in Christendom.

Outside in the bright sunlight, taking deep breaths, I replayed the scene. I saw a young woman standing alone with a middle-aged priest in a highly potent setting on the holiest day of the Christian calendar. Even then it would not have occurred to me that a sexual predator would be one of the guardians of Christ's tomb.

In the religion of my childhood, men of the cloth got married. The others, the Catholic ones, took an oath of chastity. I had never given any thought to how religious institutions dealt with the most powerful of animal drivers: the need to procreate, referred to in biblical terms as "lust."

> **Have you ever been under threat from a sexual predator?**
>
> **Were you old enough and well equipped enough to deal with the situation?**

I looked around and saw crowds of people thronging the narrow street, bearing huge wooden crosses, reciting prayers, pulsing as one in the same direction. Arab vendors lined both sides of the street, hoping for sales in holy trinkets. I could not figure out how I could possibly have been alone inside the shrine for even a few short minutes. I was safe, so I put the event to the back of my mind, catalogued as another adventure of a lady traveler.

As I sat close to the tomb of one of Christ's twelve in Santiago at the end of our pilgrimage, the events of all those years ago were suddenly quite alive and vibrant in my mind. The Good Friday encounter with a debauched priest fed into a memory of the following day in Jerusalem, when I was cornered in a back alley of the Old City.

I was on my own again. I was looking for a quick route to the Wailing Wall. Two lads offered to show me the way. They seemed kind enough, and I trusted their youth and their smiles. We were wending our way through a stone alleyway and I noticed nothing unto-ward until I realized that there was no one else in sight. I was dressed modestly, in a blue striped Balinese sarong and a white Indian shirt with long sleeves, and I carried a half-filled cloth bag slung over one shoulder. I felt safe and was enjoying the quest.

Suddenly and without warning, the boys turned on me. They moved swiftly toward me, arms outstretched, hands eager and fingers wriggling. They were babbling and grinning. I caught on each of their faces a leer not unlike the one I had seen on the face of the priest the day before. I went on instant high alert. Without a single thought entering my brain, I began to whirl like a dervish. I spun my shoulder bag around and around like an Olympic shot-putter. I roared like a lioness defending her cubs. Expletives exploded and reverberated off the stone walls. I was cornered.

My violent and unexpected response stunned them. They halted immediately and turned tail, darting back up the alley. Then they turned on me once more, scooping up some stone debris from the ground and hurling it at me. My left arm bore the brunt of the attack and showed blood, but I was too fired up with adrenaline to pay it much mind.

Then they were gone and it was over.

Sunlight highlighted the silent rubble. My legs trembled uncontrollably, my chest tightened, and my breath shortened. I was gasping for air as fright took over from fight: once in the grip of fright, I was too weak to take flight. I leaned into a shady corner where two old stone walls met and felt the coolness of the stones against my back. I tried to catch my breath, but I burst into tears instead. In the aftermath of the attack, I was like any dumb animal responding to trauma: I just wanted to crawl into my cave and lick my wounds. I had lost all interest in visiting the Wailing Wall.

When I could think again, I gave thanks to the ancestors who had bequeathed their height to me. I almost—but not quite—chuckled, re-seeing the boys' leering faces turn to terror as the wrath of Kali incarnate twirled wildly in front of them.

Jerusalem was a hotbed of religious fervor that Easter week. The atmosphere was charged with a potent mix of excited, God-driven people thrown into proximity in narrow spaces. The town was in heat. As a young woman wandering the streets of the Old City, alone in hippie attire, I must have looked like fair game for testosterone-riddled young men. It also occurred to me that the priest at the Church of the Holy Sepulchre was repeating a routine that had met with success in the past. Perhaps the very holiness of the site made it the most exciting place on earth for a sexual encounter. No previous experience in my life had ever prepared me for that thought.

I read, more recently, an autobiography of an American monk who joined an order of Indian monks in Hollywood and then spent forty years living in an ashram in France. In a footnote, he attests to having been warned by the Master that the greatest hindrance to spiritual realization was the "lust" force, or sexual drive. The monk was willing to confirm that this was so. He had witnessed the struggle and experienced it for himself. He did not belabor the point.

The two events in Jerusalem came back to me with

great clarity and all the reliability of hindsight as I sat in the pew in Santiago, waiting to pay my respects to James, son of Zebedee, friend and close disciple of Christ.

I knew where I was on the map, but I felt lost in the territory. The interior of the cathedral was richly ornamented; I wasn't really seeing it. My eyes were operating and sending messages to my brain for decoding, but this moment that I had been waiting for wasn't affecting me the way I had imagined it would.

Richard and I joined a line of people heading down to the crypt, where James's remains were purported to be and where a silver urn rested. Most people bowed, crossed themselves, paused in awe, looked closely at the urn, and slowly moved on. There were no errant priests lurking in the shadows. I followed the crowd. I felt nothing in particular. Anyway, with so many people pressing in from behind, there was no time to idle. Each person wanted just a little personal time with the saint. I was happy to comply with the needs of the person in front but had no difficulty moving on myself.

After the customary visit to the cathedral, we went to the Compostela office and lined up with lots of other pilgrims to have credencials checked and signed off on as genuine. Back in 2003, the queues were not too long, so waiting was not an arduous task. We were each asked to fill out a form stating our names, where we were from, where we had started our pilgrimage, and our reason for undertaking it.

I watched myself choosing to write Conques rather than the airport in Rodez. I had a chuckle. Still, there was no time to enter into a debate with myself about choosing approximate truth as opposed to absolute truth. I thought that if God were watching, She would understand, just as She didn't really have any objections to my not being Catholic and other such details. I struggled with the section about why I had undertaken the pilgrimage. The simple answer would have been "to go on an adventure of spiritual importance." Bilbo Baggins would have understood immediately what I meant, although he might have quibbled over the word "spiritual."

Standing there in the Compostela office with people patiently queuing up for their turn to state their truths, I had no time to process how the reason for the pilgrimage had evolved over four years and three seasons.

In truth, I don't remember what I actually wrote. If I were to be asked my answer to the question today, I would write: "To find in myself the love that permeates the whole of the universe."

I would then have to ask myself if that were true.

And how I would know. And who I would be if I continually held that thought in the forefront of my mind. And then what would happen if I suffered permanent amnesia.

**Who would you be if you
found that love within yourself?**

And held it present?

And then forgot?

We passed the "test" and were each given a Compostela. I felt very satisfied—proud even—holding my official proof of completion.

I have been a great collector of medals and certificates, credentials and awards, all my life. My high school blazer was almost lopsided with the weight of the badges and medals I wore. The Compostela represented something else to add to my long list, although I did not think of the pilgrimage in terms of an athletic or intellectual achievement.

The certificate itself was a pretty document that could slip easily inside a file folder and would not add weight to my backpack. We had them plastic-coated to protect them from wear and tear on the journey home.

Richard had booked, in advance, a small hotel on a side street that ran up to the central square where the cathedral was situated. We had dreamed many times, particularly when we were exhausted and drowning in noisy, neon-lit Spanish hostels, about treating ourselves to a couple of nights of luxury in the five-star Parador, right on the square. But by the time we reached Santiago, we were really happy to have a small room with a private bathroom and a miniature balcony. We checked into our hotel, dropped our bags with the precious Compostelas inside, and set off to explore the town.

The old streets were crowded and filled with merriment, the cathedral square no less so. Everyone's arrival was deeply personal, but the joy was tangible and shared. Sweaty, boot-shod strangers smiled complicitly at one another. The weary lay in happy bundles on the square's pavement stones. Older couples squeezed hands in quiet acknowledgment of their mutual accomplishment. Larger groups, in Christian regalia, sang boisterous victory songs in different languages. It was all a jolly mishmash of pilgrims, holidaymakers, and tourists taking pictures of each other, of everything, of anyone; it didn't much matter which.

The exuberance I witnessed and belonged to outside the cathedral contrasted dramatically with the silent extravagance I felt little part of inside its walls and under its vaults. However, the sense of not belonging did not stop me from embracing the opportunity to attend the daily midday mass for pilgrims.

The cathedral was crammed to capacity. The *botafumeiro*—a giant incense burner—was lit and swung vigorously into action by eight *tiraboleiros* dressed in traditional, long red robes. As it swung higher and higher, it cast off huge clouds of perfumed smoke over the heads of the entire congregation. Someone told me it was an effective way of fumigating unwashed crowds of pilgrims, and that in the Middle Ages there were those who believed it prevented the spread of bubonic plague.

I had a good view of its trajectory but quietly noted that if the chain should break and the eighty kilograms of gleaming gold and silver should crash on the heads of the faithful, I would probably, given where I sat, be saved. It was a comforting thought. The incantations and prayers of the priests in their vibrant green-and-gold robes, the muscular, sweaty action being wrought upon the *botafumeiro* by the men in red, and the smoky, perfumed atmosphere all made for a heady and spectacular performance. I was really impressed and glad I had not missed it, despite my misgivings about the institution that hosted it. The ritual was a fitting closure to the last four years of my life on the road with Richard.

But the journey was not over yet.

The Witch at the End of the Earth

While the visit to the saint's tomb inside the cathedral had not been an earth-shaking experience for me personally, the arrival in Santiago itself had been far more emotionally charged than I had expected. I had always imagined Fisterra to be my true destination; at the same time, I was surprised by how joyful and sad I had felt when we reached Santiago and had our journey recognized as a true pilgrimage. I had always imagined that the pilgrimage would end in Fisterra, where I would stand, watching the sun disappear over a flat line, confirming the ancient belief that the earth itself was flat, stable, and the center of the universe. I had entertained myself with the certainty that I would run no risk of the church's persecuting me for a heretical belief in Galileo and Copernicus's theory of heliocentrism as it would have done half a millennium ago.

Whatever the scientific reality, the historical import, or my imaginings about the place, I had always wanted to be part of the pilgrim tradition of burning my old clothes and casting my walk-weary boots into the ocean from the rocky promontory at the farthest point west in Galicia. I was in love with the romance of bowing to the setting sun in the west before turning symbolically and literally toward the east to embrace the rising sun and a new life post-pilgrimage.

After two days' rest in Santiago, we packed up and continued walking west to Fisterra. The guidebook said that it would take us three days to get there, but that meant walking thirty to thirty-five kilometers a day. We were well used to twenty-five and could go thirty at a stretch, but we had no desire to hurry or hurt ourselves, so we planned on covering the distance in four days. What we did not plan on, however, was the weather.

We completed the first day out of Santiago easily enough. That night, torrential, monsoon-like rain came down, continuing in full force the following morning. We were dressed and ready to set off, albeit very reluctantly, when Richard said, "What about taking a taxi the first twelve kilometers? It may stop raining, and anyway, it will reduce the amount of time getting soaked."

I remembered our April 2000 vow. We had declared that we would stop and wait or go home if we could not carry on. We had also promised ourselves that no one else would carry our *besaces* if we could not.

I looked out the windows of our hostel and watched the heavens empty. I could practically feel, in my bones, the bleak trudge out of town, the chill of sopping-wet clothes, the squelch of soggy boots. I thought of the further three days of walking and the difficulty of drying clothes if the rain continued. But uppermost in my mind was the thought of breaking our four-year vow. In a nanosecond, it seemed, my mind provided me with a counterargument: the pilgrimage was officially completed. We had certificates to prove it.

I said yes.

Richard ordered a taxi and we climbed aboard, sliding our backpacks into the trunk and settling down on the back seat for our first ride intra-pilgrimage.

In the time it took to drive the twelve kilometers from our hostel, the rain had stopped and the sun was shining mockingly. The driver stopped his taxi at a crossroads in the middle of nowhere the moment his gauge registered the requested twelve kilometers.

Not a soul in sight.

Not a house to be seen.

Flat fields.

Long grass.

Nothing.

Just four roads stretching out far behind, far in front, far to the right, and far to the left.

We got out of the taxi. We removed our backpacks from the trunk and were hoisting them up onto our shoulders with a familiar swing when my eye caught a movement to my right. I turned and saw an old woman, dressed in black, advancing rapidly toward us, brandishing an umbrella.

She shouts words I don't recognize. The tone is full of venom. The gap between her and me gets smaller and smaller. I see she is very old. Her face is weather-beaten, her skin heavily lined. A black scarf covers her head, tied under her chin. Her back is bent. Her clothes are dark and patched.

She is upon us.

She shrieks like a banshee.

She raises her umbrella and brings it down with a thwack.

It hits my right shoulder.

She is too old and weak for it to cause me any pain. In any case I am too astounded to retaliate. Richard watches, spellbound. Her vitriol is for me, not him, and she continues to douse me with it. I turn my head toward the taxi driver, looking for an explanation. He is looking at his feet and his shoulders have slumped.

"What is she saying?" I gasp, raising my arm to deflect another assault from her rolled umbrella.

"False pilgrims! Cheats!" he mutters without lifting his eyes from his shoelaces.

And THAT thwacks me behind the knees and lands full-force in my gut. The driver looks up, sees the look on my face, remembers he hasn't been paid yet, and shoos her away as one would a rabid dog.

Then she is gone.

She disappears into thin air. There is no one to be seen to the left, to the right, behind, or in front.

We pay the driver. He gets back in his cab, turns around, and drives back the way he came.

We set off down an empty road. Nothing but the soft sound of boots on bitumen.

After that, my mind was messy. The hag had screeched words that cut into my sense of self: someone who kept her promises—someone who had sufficient self-discipline to abide by her word. My shoulder was unscathed, but my pride had suffered a real blow. I saw what she saw: two people getting out of a taxi, wearing all the signs of the pilgrim. No use proclaiming four years and three seasons of diligence. No use whipping out the Compostela. No point arguing honesty when caught in the act. I heard the judge declare me guilty of letting the side down. I heard his mallet smash down on his wooden bench in one final stroke, leaving no room for further discussion. Once sentenced, I felt my feet begin to drag along the road, my stride slow, and my shoulders begin to ache.

A little later, I was able to see the scene from another perspective. The serious slipped into the risible. Could a guilty conscience seriously materialize in the form of a black crone shrieking insults? Was I just beaten up by the Wicked Witch of the West wielding an umbrella on a deserted road in the middle of nowhere? A long way from Kansas and Dorothy's red shoes.

There was no rational explanation for the old woman's sudden appearance or its immaculate timing.

After trying once to hitch a ride up on the high plateau road in April 2000, we had never once been tempted to break our personal vow of walking the whole way and carrying our own backpacks. And yet the one time we took a taxi, an exception we had rationalized as being post-Santiago and had justified as having been provoked by inclement weather, we were accused by a stranger of being cheats. The accusations were directed at me, not Richard. I took to seeing the witch as an interfering biddy at best, and at worst as evil.

But that was before I learned something about

witches. The word derives from the Old English *wicce* (feminine) and *wicca* (masculine) and is thought to have meant "wise one" and to be associated with fortune-telling and teaching based on foreknowledge. The hag who appeared as if by magic revealed the crack in the pristine image I sought to project to the world and wished I could fool myself with too. The "world" was not witness to this lapse in perfection, so the witch was only revealing me to myself. She was screeching, "And your flaw shall make you whole!"

A few years after completing the Camino, I bought a crystal that dangled on a silver chain and had a little amethyst at the end of it. I bought it at a health and well-being fair. Most of all I bought it because it had a flaw, one that did not detract from its elegant shape and pristine smooth surface: a tiny crack, visible only if you hold it up to the light. It is its flaw that reminds me of my humanity. It is the crack that lets the light in.

We completed the four-day walk to Fisterra with dry boots and easy minds. My judge and I walked peaceably together. We were ready to embrace the setting sun at the end of the earth.

What question could I possibly
ask you about strange old women
who appear out of nowhere, uninvited,
then disappear into thin air?

Do you have a flaw that bothers you
more than any other?

The End of the Earth

After the encounter with the strange old woman and the introspection it had provoked, the rest of the journey to the end of the earth was comparatively uneventful. The sun shone consistently, for one thing.

We followed a shoreline of beautiful sheltered bays, all of them invitations to forget walking and just loaf on the sand and swim all day.

We didn't.

But we did take off our boots to paddle in the cool waters of one of the bays. We met a guy walking the Camino with his short-legged dog. He told us he had had to carry him some of the way. *That's love*, I thought.

I remember loving a cat I had when I was small. We called her Blackie. I don't know how long she was in the family, but I remember how sad I felt the day she died. It must have been winter, because there was a fire burning in the hearth and Blackie was curled up in a basket beside it. I didn't recognize the difference between sleep and death. I don't know who told me that Blackie was dead. I can't ask my father, because he is dead himself now; my mother doesn't remember Blackie.

I was touched by the tender look on the guy's face as he watched his little dog scampering wildly around on the beach and told us that his four stumpy legs couldn't always go the distance on the road day after day.

We had met Christian groups transporting disabled people in sedan chairs over mountain passes and along treacherous gullies on their way to Santiago. It was the spirit of the Way.

It made sense to me that the guy on the beach would have picked up his dog and carried him in his arms when he saw that his little companion was too tired and sore to continue trotting alongside him. I had only ever loved one other animal like that. It was another cat, one that I had when I was much older. She was a shade of marmalade, and I took her everywhere with me. I took her to the country for an outing and let her out of her basket to go explore the bush. She had never been in the wild before, and I did not know enough about cats to know I had just signed her death warrant. I eventually found her and took her home. She started frothing at the mouth a few days later. I took her to the vet, and he whispered in my ear that it was rabies. The vet kept her in a cage separated from the other animals. I went back to see her the following day before they put her down. I cried then more hopelessly than I could ever imagine crying for the loss of a human life.

Do you know what I mean?

We left the man and his dog to their adventure together while we continued on ours.

Eventually we got there. The very last stamp in my credencial is dated August 30, 2003, and it has the scallop shell inside a stylized hostel: the logo of the Albergue de Fisterra in black ink above the date.

We dropped our backpacks at the hostel, secured a bunk for the night, then made our way to the cape at the end of the earth to await sunset.

We were not alone standing on the rocky promontory, waiting to capture the embers of the day on film. It was a solemn occasion, gazing out to sea with no further land in sight. The sun was slowly making Its way toward the distant flat line separating sea from sky. There was a bronze sculpture of an old boot, toes forward, welded to the rocks. There were other pairs of well-worn boots, strategically placed on barren rock against an endless ocean and a changing sky, for the emblematic shot that said, "This is it. We're here. Nowhere else to go!"

There were black spots on the rocks closer to where sea met rock and crashed. They were the charred remnants of clothes burned there by pilgrims of an age that predated twenty-first-century environmental concerns. These pilgrims had cast their old clothes into a ritual fire, stripping themselves of their past. Thus cleansed, according to tradition, they could begin a new life.

We were as far west as the land would take us, and as the sun slowly relinquished its hold on the day, the sky responded in shades from molten marigold to stewed cherry. When the sun finally slipped over the edge of sea-sky, we were left staring at a vast expanse of luminous twilight blue. We stood in awe inside the fading remnants of our last day until night enfolded us in black dazzling with myriads of diamonds.

The palms of my hands opened naturally to the night in gratitude. They came together slowly before my heart in reverence. I felt a lump in my throat and tears in my eyes. All those who had stayed to watch the passing of the day stood in silent wonder, in communion, receiving nature's blessing—God's grace. This was my cathedral. This was where prayer made sense.

Where is your house of worship —your cathedral?

We turned around, left the promontory, and followed the trail of silent visitors along the dirt track that had led us out to the edge of the world. Some climbed back into the vehicles they had left at the end of the road; others walked the four kilometers back to town. A few, like us, returned to the Albergue de Fisterra, which was closer to the track than to town.

The following day we set out to accomplish the final act of our pilgrimage: to divest ourselves of our old clothes in a ritualistic way.

There had been a gigantic oil spill off the coast of Spain, causing massive damage to beaches and wildlife. Armies of volunteers were still trying to clean up the mess. It was therefore totally inappropriate that we should try to burn our clothes or cast them into the sea.

What we did instead was go down to the sandy

beach on the northern side of the cape in the morning, when the sun was well up in the sky. We removed our boots and socks, leaving the boots in obvious view next to our backpacks on the sand. We stuffed our socks into our trouser pockets and sidled barefoot down to the shoreline. I looked around furtively, checking that no one was watching us, before surreptitiously removing my socks from my trouser pocket and placing them in the water. I watched their contours sway like seaweed tugged and delivered with each small movement of tide-on-shore. Then they were gone, sucked out and under by the force of each wave. I offered a prayer of thanks for having completed the journey and asked for forgiveness for adding pollution to an already overburdened sea. I felt guilty, but my desire to complete a symbolic act at the end of the earth overruled my conscience.

There were some small groups of people sitting around bonfires on the beach. I wondered if they were burning their old clothes or debris from the oil spill or just boiling water for tea. I didn't approach anyone to find out. I felt that the easy camaraderie of the Way had ended in the hostel the night before, when we'd reached the end of the road. Right or wrong, I felt that the familiarity of sharing walkways with strangers was over.

We sat together, alone in our thoughts, for a while

on the beach. We watched two black fins slide smoothly from one side of the beach to the other, close to the shoreline. They didn't soar, curve, and dip like those of dolphins at play. *Sharks*, I thought. *Plenty to prey on.*

The sky was slightly overcast by then, and there was a vague chill in the air. I had a strong sense that it was time to leave the beach and the path.

We walked back to town. I bought a scallop shell at a local market. We had walked over a thousand kilometers on the Camino, but it wasn't until our journey was over that I thought to purchase this emblem. It would later find its place on an altar in our living room, propped up against a Buddha head and behind a statuette of Krishna and next to an icon of the Madonna and Child: a suitably eclectic assemblage for a middle-aged woman in the twenty-first century.

I took pictures of the colorful little fishing boats in the harbor of Fisterra that I would later have blown up and framed. I would give one of them to my dad, lover of sea and boats. I was collecting tangible memories. To give or to keep. Last-minute things. As if I wasn't quite ready to let go, to turn around, to go home.

We eventually took a bus back to Santiago, then a train to Pamplona, then another bus back across the Pyrenees to the beach in Hendaye, where we rested for a few more days before taking a train back to Paris.

The pilgrimage to Saint James in Santiago was over, but really we would complete it the following year in the place where it had all started: Conques.

PART 6   FRANCE
Sur les Pas de St Jacques
CONQUES
2004   SUMMER

Endings and Beginnings

We had been to Santiago and to the end of the earth. But we had started out from an airport and not a sanctified point of departure. After four years of seasonal walking over longer and longer periods of time, Richard and I felt like old hands, and we were reluctant to finish this chapter of our lives without closing the gestalt—closing the circle. We wanted to start out from the cathedral in Le Puy-en-Velay and finish in Conques, where we had taken part in the Palm Sunday mass for pilgrims in April 2000. It was there that we had experienced for the first time what walking the Way might mean as a spiritual undertaking. We also wanted to share a little of what we had lived with some close friends, Gill and Daniel. Our ending would be their be-ginning. That felt right, and they were keen to join us.

Our roles were clearly defined from the outset: Richard brought out the maps and talked distances and accommodation. I was helpful on drip-dry clothes, lightweight equipment, and tea.

Have you gone on an adventure with good friends?

How did it start out?

How did it end?

The four of us met up in the old town of Le Puy-en-Velay in July 2004. The exact date is unrecorded because Richard and I were no longer collecting stamps in our credencials. We had our Compostela certificates and needed no further proof of good intention.

Setting out, I wondered how our friendship would stand up to ten days of walking over rough terrain. While neither Richard nor I knew this section of the Way, we did know the codes and rituals of pilgrims. I hoped neither of us would flaunt our experience like the know-it-all harpy who had fueled my fury in Sahagún. I hoped Richard had taken into account that our friends, while prepared to rough it a bit, might not want to forgo hot showers, comfortable beds, and hot meals at the end of each day. I was conscious that lack of privacy had been a big challenge for me initially. The four of us had known each other for many years, and we had one essential quality in common: the capacity to listen. I was relying on that and our shared good humor to carry us through any tough moments.

We were pretty tired by the time we arrived in Le Puy-en-Velay. We had driven from Paris, left the car in a car park in Conques, and then taken a taxi to Le Puy. The route that took a couple of hours to cover in a taxi was going to take us the next ten days to walk.

Le Puy was picturesque, perched atop an ancient volcano and graced with a magnificent medieval cathedral. The cobblestone streets at both the top and the bottom of the town were lined with houses with red roofs, mullion windows, and brightly colored facades. We dined on the local specialty of lentils at the top of the town and then walked down to the bottom for dessert in an ice cream parlor. It had been raining, and we were the only ones out on the terrace. Thirty-four different flavors of ice cream were advertised in bold lettering, with no mention of *plombières*—candied fruit soaked in kirsch. Daniel's favorite.

The waitress comes to take our order.

"Could I have a plombières?" Daniel asks.

"Sorry, sir, we don't have that flavor," she responds.

"What flavors do you have, then?" Daniel asks.

The waitress reels off all thirty-four with practiced disinterest.

"I'll have the plombières," Daniel says, smiling. He doesn't bat an eyelid and shows no sign of mockery. We gape in astonishment.

The waitress pauses, emits a patient sigh, and says, "We don't have any, sir."

Daniel, genuinely disappointed says, "Oh, what flavors do you have, then?" The waitress just looks at him, her shoulders sag a little, and she begins her litany of flavors once again.

The three of us erupt in gales of laughter and shout in unison, "He'll have the plombières!"

Daniel wakes up, realizes what has happened, and says sheepishly, "But I really like candied fruit ice cream soaked in kirsch."

From then on, the standard joke among us was to say, "He'll have the plombières, please!"—regardless of whether it appeared on the menu. In fact, not once in those ten days did we ever find any mention of candied fruit ice cream soaked in kirsch, anywhere. It didn't prevent us from asking for it for Daniel and then roaring with laughter when we were politely refused. And he never let us down: he always succeeded in looking disappointed.

Early the following morning, after receiving the pilgrims' blessing, we stepped out of the darkness of the cathedral, passed through its central archway, and descended the sixty steps to begin our journey together.

I don't remember what was said during the benedictory service, but I do remember writing a little prayer on a slip of paper and putting it in a box. I don't remember what I wrote, but I do remember the feeling of belonging to an age-old tradition of private conversations with God scribbled on bits of paper and thrust into ancient boxes. I felt at ease taking part in the tradition.

The landscape, shaped by ancient volcanoes, was new to me, and beautifully picturesque in the early morning light. I looked back from time to time at the town, its cathedral perched precariously and surrounded by toy-size colorful block houses slowly diminishing in size as we walked on.

I noticed quite quickly that my backpack was no lighter than it had ever been—my penchant for a little luxury was undiminished. I knew how to measure my effort after four years of practice, but I had grown used to silence. The boisterous departure of many groups of new pilgrims promised fun and companionship but also threatened distraction. It would not be the first time in my life that I noted that when my mouth was at work, my eyes ceased to see and my ears were exclusively occupied with the sounds and flavors of words: mine or my companions'.

The first two days passed uneventfully. On day three we walked to the Domaine du Sauvage, in Chanaleilles. We approached it via a long, winding gravel road. From a distance I could just make out a cluster of old stone farmhouses nestling in a tuck in the road. I read on arrival that stone buildings had occupied this site since the days of the Knights Templar in the Middle Ages.

Foolishly, Richard and I chose a room on the ground floor with just four single beds. We chose privacy over practicality, forgetting that heat rises and thick stone walls don't hold summer heat once the sun goes down. It would have been wiser to have slept upstairs in the dormitory, closer to the warmth of the kitchen.

We bought fresh farm eggs, slices of cured ham, and homemade bread for our breakfast the following morning. In the evening, we joined the other pilgrims around a long trestle table for a communal meal of lentils and vegetables, all deliciously stewed in a huge pot and served with fresh bread straight from the oven. Our friends were delighted with the atmosphere and shared in the inevitable conversations around the number of kilometers covered, future places to stay, and people met along the Way.

Light slowly relinquished its hold on the day, the sun surrendering itself in a fiery mass over a hilly horizon and disappearing into a dark night filled with twinkling stars. We were all ready to slip into a deep, peaceful sleep after a long day of walking and a wholesome meal. We closed our bedroom door and climbed into our sleeping bags: Daniel near the tiny window high up the outside wall, Gill next to him, then Richard and me closest to the door.

Almost as soon as the light was out, Gill began to snore. This was not a polite excuse for a snore. This was an operatic version. This was a star baritone at La Scala. The sound had Wagnerian dimensions.

No one seemed to want to take responsibility for waking Gill. For Richard and me, it was as if we had arrived at some unspoken agreement: if Daniel didn't do it, it was no one else's place. We lay there wrapped in the chilly, damp arms of the night. The beds sagged in the middle, and Wagner continued to bounce off the stone walls.

The night wore on. And on. And on.

Gill awoke fresh and without knowledge of her night's performance. Daniel awoke with a raging head-ache and flu-like symptoms. Richard said nothing, and I silently decided to suggest separate sleeping arrange-ments at our next stop. I didn't know how many sleepless nights would be needed to put an old friendship in jeopardy, but I wasn't willing to find out either.

Daniel and Richard were introverts and Gill an extrovert. I moved happily back and forth between both ways of being. Introverts and extroverts don't always approve of each other's behavior in public. Typically, Gill liked to think out loud and needed an audience to do it well. Her ideas, like those of most extroverts, evolved almost from one thought and one phrase to the next and at times risked contradicting themselves. Richard, on the other hand, did all his thinking on the inside and very often forgot that he hadn't actually given voice to his ideas, which sometimes left others perplexed and him feeling misunderstood. He tended to dismiss Gill's enthusiastically half-formulated ideas, because he didn't have the patience to wait until they became full-fledged points of view. Gill mostly respected Richard's silences but didn't always interpret them well. Daniel and I provided comic relief when tension arose, which it did when we were physically tired.

We were resting down by a river in the late afternoon. Gill was talking animatedly about some work she was doing with a client. We shared the same profession, so I was mildly interested, and it wasn't costing me any extra energy to listen. I wasn't taking in many of the details. Daniel was lying contentedly on his back in the grass, not really paying attention to what was being said. Richard for some reason decided to call Gill to task on what she was asserting as fact.

Years of putting politicians on the spot with politely delivered questions that nevertheless had serrated edges had made Richard a successful journalist but not necessarily a tolerant friend. His questions sliced into Gill's discourse. She rose competitively to the challenge, and the joust began. They shared middle-class British backgrounds, he on his mother's side and she on both sides. Each was an only child. They kept the conversation on a deathly jovial footing. I felt nervous. I did not enjoy anything approaching conflict between friends. I preferred to keep my mouth shut or find an amusing way to defuse tension in a relationship. They threw remarks at each other with much feigned humor, and neither seemed willing to let the other have the last word.

Daniel, being a native Frenchman, could switch off, as all this was taking place in the very best of British English. I recognized not only the journalist in Richard but also his French side. Dispute was second nature, and I rather fancied he was enjoying himself.

When it was over and no one had won and it was time to move on again, I had a bad taste in my mouth. I hoped that no irreparable damage had been done to the relationship. Fortunately, Gill was not a bearer of grudges, and Richard had his inner cave to crawl into to lick his wounds.

Like the sleepless night in the Domaine du Sauvage, the clash was never mentioned again.

When you see that two people you're close to are arguing, what do you do?

We walked on to the huge plateaus of Aubrac. The cows on the Aubrac pass were magnificent.

Caramel hides
ambling
under a sky
of skin-tight blue.

Muddy hooves
squelching
over rain-soaked turf.

Emerald, brown
stony track
wending its way
between bovine eyes.

We treated ourselves to a night in a hotel at the top of the pass, ate foie gras, and drank deliciously sweet wine. We slept in comfortable beds in separate rooms and enjoyed a continental breakfast before hitting the road again. The day that followed this brief recline into luxury seemed impossibly long and reminded me of how I had felt leaving the comfort of the hotel in Burgos two years before: disgruntled! I still found transitions psychologically and physically difficult. No change!

To pass the time and reduce the sense of its passing too slowly, Gill and I entertained ourselves by singing my old school hymn, "Jerusalem," at the top our voices to a farmyard full of disinterested pigs. It was riotously funny for the two of us and dismally dull for Richard and Daniel. We provided the pigs with an unsolicited encore of "God Save the Queen" and once again failed to impress them. We spent a silly amount of energy roaring with laughter and forced Daniel and Richard to put as much distance as possible between them and us. The extroverted part of myself joined up with Gill's best party-self, and neither of us gave a damn about the din we were making. I figured I would never pass that way again and that the locals, if they were in any way concerned, would just put the choir practice for a pig audience down to some kind of foreign eccentricity.

We were covering twenty to twenty-five kilometers

a day, with the longest stretch taking us through Estaing and across its well-known old bridge. And on that particular day the rain bucketed down. We arrived at our hotel drenched to the bone and shoved balled-up newspaper deep into our sopping boots, praying that they would dry out overnight. In all the walking we had done previously, we had always managed to set off with dry boots the following day. This time we were out of luck.

The following morning, we squeezed our dry stocking feet into cold, damp leather or Gore-Tex boots and tried to look cheery about the life of a pilgrim. Daniel's cold had not improved, and not having any time to rest was wearing down his morale. Starting the day with cold, wet feet didn't help. He didn't complain, but we could see his body was suffering with each extra kilometer he willed it to walk. He coughed a lot and ran a temperature for a good part of the ten days we spent together. His face was permanently pale, and he ran out of steam very quickly on the hill climbs. I think he was grateful that we kept him going by imposing regular stops.

Seen from the outside, Gill's initiation into the Way was full of energetic chatter and bonhomie with fellow walkers, whereas Daniel's initiation looked more like a via dolorosa.

On the day before we reached Conques, I crossed paths with a fellow coach I had not seen for four years. Our last encounter was at the stèle or stone cross of Saint-Palais. Then as now, we were headed in opposite directions. And this meeting was equally unexpected and as unlikely as the first one. It was really odd and, I thought, providential that I should be meeting him just as we were preparing to close the gestalt—as if he were part of that process.

On the earlier occasion, Richard and I had been standing contemplating the stèle, which marks the meeting point of the three main French pilgrim routes before they become one in Saint-Jean-Pied-de-Port, at the foot of the mountain pass into Spain. A guy around our age had approached us. He was dressed like us, but he was traveling light. He stood there with us for a few minutes as we all looked out at the stèle. Then he looked straight at me and said, "Are you a coach?"

I wheeled around to make sure that he was in fact addressing me.

"Yes," I replied.

"Is your name Lynne Burney?" he continued.

Now I was truly dumbfounded.

"Yes," I said again.

He laughed and didn't seem to find it the least surprising that he should know me, or at least my name. I, on the other hand, was blown away. I felt like a celebrity. No audience and no applause but definitely a taste of fame. It was a delicious moment. I tried to appear blasé, as if I were used to meeting my fans at stone monoliths in the middle of the French countryside. The kid in me wanted to strut or swagger or both. For a moment I felt more famous than Richard, the journalist from *L'Express*. He may have had hundreds of readers, but I had one fan right here now, in person, and he knew my name and what I looked like.

I was around six years old when I first dreamed of standing in the spotlight, center stage, in a pink tutu, receiving accolades: me, Pavlova—all grace and swan and stardom.

My mother sent me to ballet classes when I was eight, but I hated them. I felt silly. I wanted to run fast and jump far. My hair was too short for me to be a ballerina anyway.

I don't know where my Pavlova dreams came from, but at that moment, there at the meeting of the three paths, I was six years old again, reveling in an imaginary spotlight minus the pink and the pointe shoes.

Four years later and just before Conques, I don't remember what we said to each other, but I know we didn't talk about coaching. I had not seen him once in the four-year interim since our meeting at the stèle of

Saint-Palais, but we chatted like old friends for a few minutes before parting ways again. Unexpected encounters were to be expected along the Way.

We made it to Conques for the second time after four years, three seasons, and ten days.

Two things happened there. Both were unexpected.

Whereas in 2000 we had stayed at a little hotel in the center of the old town, this time we stayed at the Sainte-Foy Abbey in the pilgrims' dormitory. We dumped our bags and headed off to the abbey church, where for me it had all begun.

It was inside this church that I had first felt the profundity of what we were undertaking. It may have been the white habits of the Prémontré monks. It may have been the simplicity of their blessing offered to all departing pilgrims—a crust of bread. It may have been the austerity of the filtered light through the stained glass windows blessed by the hand of Pierre Soulages. It may have been the advent of Palm Sunday. Whatever it was, this church had left its indelible mark on me.

I entered it with a sense of awe. My heart rate rose and my legs trembled. I had a sense of moving toward completion—of closing the gestalt.

There were many people wandering the aisles and lingering in the various nooks of the church. Their voices rumbled and murmured within the stone walls. I had lost sight of Richard and our two friends. I was alone among the jostle and rustle of summer clothes.

And there, in one of the nooks, chiseled in wood, polished but not smooth, his name: Saint Jacques—Santiago—Saint James. It was as if I were seeing him for the first time. The sobs came from deep inside me, shaking my shoulders and turning my breath into small gulping movements. I sank to the floor and leaned against one of the many pillars holding up the edifice. Had there been fewer people or more space, I would have dropped to my knees and slid to full length on my stomach, stretching my arms in supplication toward the tiny wooden feet of Saint James—the one who had traveled with Christ. I was overcome with love, with gratitude, with fullness, with grief.

It was over. The gestalt was closed.

Almost.

Sometime later I left the church and walked out into the late afternoon sunshine. I felt emotionally drained and disinclined to engage in a discussion about where to eat that night or what time we should get going the following morning. I wandered the old cobblestone streets on my own and eventually made my way back to the hostel dormitory.

I found Daniel engaged in a conversation with a girl setting out to Santiago. I didn't interrupt but sat quietly on my bed, idly curious. They were discussing weather prospects for the coming week and the likelihood of rain. She expressed doubt that her lightweight jacket would be effective if she got caught in heavy rain over a long period.

C'mon, girl, are you serious? That thing wouldn't keep you dry under a dripping tap! I chuckled to myself without actually saying anything to that effect. I had already classified her as a new-age hippie: idealistic and ill-equipped for a journey on foot over 1,500 kilometers in all weather.

Then I witnessed an act of simple Christian kindness that touched me to the quick. It was this gesture that fully closed the circle and brought the journey to a close in the fullness of the spirit of the Way and its power to transform souls.

Daniel and the girl are facing each other. Because his first language is French and hers is German, their English is simple in form. Daniel turns, takes a few steps over to his bunk, plunges his hand into his backpack, and returns to the conversation, holding his waterproof cape.

"Please take this. I do not need it now. I am stopping

here. You will need it for your journey," he says, smiling.

"I cannot take this from you," she says, touched and a little embarrassed. She is new to the path.

"Please, I want you to have it," he says, holding the cape out to her, still smiling.

She hesitates. There is a pause. A suspension.

"Thank you," she finally says, holding out her arms to receive the cape.

It is done with grace. The gesture is simplicity itself. It is sincere. I am its witness.

Coda

The world from which this story is being told is a world that brutally shut down in response to a virus in the first quarter of 2020. It is a world still trying to etch new contours out of the chaos that ensued. Collectively, we are transitioning into an as yet unrecognizable world. There is no way back. But we can remember. I remember the year of COVID-19:

> The people stayed home.
> The animals went out.
> The kids grew up.
> The flowers bloomed
> and the seasons turned.
> People went bankrupt.
> Businesses changed.
> The kids went to school online.
> The elderly lined up
> to die
> for lack of ventilators.
> The planes

stayed down.
The numbers infected
stayed up
with no vaccine in sight.
And we talked
and talked
and talked some more.
We needed to know
who was safe
and
who was not.
We came together
like never before.
And that was the year of COVID.
19 was its number.
Stable, they said.
But what will 20 be like?
We know what 2020 was like.
Was there an 18 we didn't know about,
when Corona was just a beer?
And here in the middle,
who knows anything anymore?
Between fake and real,
dying has clarity,
and purpose,
and certainty.

While the contours of confinement
blur us,
make us messy,
uneasy,
unsure.
But here we are.
Together.
Close as we have never been,
in our deep separation.

These words came easily to me, early on the morning of April 4, 2020. I had no need to think or struggle. Some things are just obvious. Producing the words required no more effort than simply following their direction until they announced that they were finished and there was nothing more to add. Now they belong to everyone.

On the contrary, telling the tale of my journey to the tomb of Saint James in Santiago with Richard, my then partner, now husband, was an effort! In recalling events that took place twenty years ago, I was hampered by the loss of the dairies I faithfully wrote in every night of those four years and three seasons of walking. Writing was a transformative process, not always comfortable or easy. The caterpillar who is happily munching her way through leaves sees no reason to change anything, in spite of the odd predator or two; nature calls her to make herself a chrysalis. She heads into the unknown and unseen; she loses her former shape, purpose, and size. She emerges as a transformed creature: a butterfly. And there is no going back. Like the butterfly, I carry the memory in my cells of my "me" prior to walking the Way. But, like the rest of the world, I can never return to the innocence and leaf-munching life of the caterpillar—the world before COVID. Today, we collectively experience a great deal of uncertainty about what our "butterflies" will end up being. Here I look back to a simpler time and see clearly that the pilgrimage to Saint James in Santiago has wrought great changes in me.

Acknowledgements

I have come to understand that writing a book is a collective effort. I am deeply grateful to James Navé (*www.jamesnave.com*), American poet, storyteller and manuscript coach who guided me so generously through the making of this book. His observations, questions and advice led me to find real joy in telling this tale. Further, he introduced me to his friend and colleague, Janet Byrne, a highly skilled professional editor who, with kindness and a keen eye, whipped the manuscript into a publishable state. I have learned so much from them both. Thank you.

A special thank you to Jennifer de Gandt for her unfailing personal and professional support for over twenty years. I bow to your wisdom.

To Kris Harbert-Hamon, good friend and first reader, I say thank you for your concluding remark: "Fabulous!"—a word which will always make my heart soar!

To Ysée Mathieu and my husband, Richard de Vendeuil, a huge thank you for all the hours that have gone into translating the story into French so that my bilingual professional public will get a chance to enjoy it as well.

And to all those others I have not named who were willing to respond to my requests for information, advice and support. You all helped! Thank you.

About the Author

Lynne Burney was born in Christchurch, New Zealand, in 1952. She has lived and worked in France for the past forty-two years. She has been an executive coach for more than twenty-five years and has run her own school—LKB School of Coaching—in Paris for the past twenty-two years. She has a son and two beautiful granddaughters.

She said yes to her life partner, Richard, in February, 2000 when he suggested a pilgrimage to the feet of Saint James in Santiago, Spain. She said yes again when he asked her to marry him in 2016. They live in Paris.